Editors

Mary S. Jones, M.A.

Cristina Krysinski, M. Ed.

Editor in Chief

Karen J. Goldfluss, M.S. Ed.

Creative Director

Sarah M. Smith

Cover Artist

Diem Pascarella

Art Coordinator

Renée McElwee

Imaging

Ariyanna Simien

Publisher

Mary D. Smith, M.S. Ed..

packets - Homework
for 3 packets
Gael, Cameron,
+ David
pages - 29, 30, 31,
32, 33, 34. 45, 46,
47 48, 49, 50

The lessons and activities in each unit have been correlated to Common Core State Standards for English Language Arts. Correlations charts are provided on pages 7 and 8 and can also be found at *http://www.teachercreated.com/standards*.

Teacher Created Resources

6421 Industry Way

Westminster, CA 92683

www.teachercreated.com

ISBN: 978-1-4206-8031-7

© 2014 Teacher Created Resources

Made in U.S.A.

Table of Contents

What Is Comprehension?

Comprehension is a cognitive process. It involves the capacity of the mind to understand, using logic and reasoning. For students, it should be more than a process of trying to guess the answers to formal exercises after reading text. Students need to know **how to think about and make decisions about a text before, during, and after reading it**.

Teaching Comprehension

Comprehension skills can and should be developed by teaching students strategies that are appropriate to a particular comprehension skill and then providing opportunities for them to discuss and practice applying those strategies to the texts they read. These strategies can be a series of clearly defined steps to follow.

Students need to understand that it is the **process**—not the product—that is more important. In other words, they need to understand how it is done before they are required to demonstrate that they can do it.

Higher-order comprehension skills are within the capacity of young students, but care needs to be taken to ensure that the level and language of the text is appropriately assigned.

The text can be read to the students. When introducing comprehension strategies to students, the emphasis should be on the discussion, and the comprehension activities should be completed orally before moving on to supported and then independent practice and application. The lessons in this book are scaffolded to accommodate this process.

Note: Some students may not be able to complete the activities independently. For those students, additional support should be provided as they work through the activities within each unit.

Before students start the activities in this book, discuss the concepts of paragraphs and stanzas. Note that the paragraphs in each reading passage or stanza have been numbered for easy reference as students complete activities.

The terms *skills* and *strategies* are sometimes confused. The following explanation provides some clarification of how the two terms are used in this book.

Skills relate to competent performance and come from knowledge, practice, and aptitude.

Strategies involve planning and tactics.

In other words, we can teach *strategies* that will help students acquire specific comprehension *skills*.

Twelve comprehension skills are introduced in this book. Information about these skills and how the units and lessons are designed to explore them are provided on pages 4 – 6.

Metacognitive Strategies

Metacognitive strategies, which involve teaching students how to think about thinking, are utilized in developing the twelve comprehension skills taught in this book. Metacognitive strategies are modeled and explained to students for each skill. As this is essentially an oral process, teachers are encouraged to elaborate on and discuss the explanations provided on each "Learning Page." The activities on these pages allow students to talk about the different thought processes they would use in answering each question.

Students will require different levels of support before they are able to work independently to comprehend, make decisions about text, and choose the best answer in multiple-choice questions. This support is provided within each unit lesson by including guided practice, modeled practice using the metacognitive processes, and assisted practice using hints and clues.

Comprehension Strategies

The exercises in this book have been written—not to test—but to stimulate and challenge students and to help them develop their thinking processes through modeled metacognitive strategies, discussion, and guided and independent practice. There are no trick questions, but many require and encourage students to use logic and reasoning.

Particularly in the higher-order comprehension skills, there may be more than one acceptable answer. The reader's prior knowledge and experience will influence some of his or her decisions about the text. Teachers may choose to accept an answer if a student can justify and explain his or her choice. Therefore, some of the answers provided should not be considered prescriptive but more of a guide and a basis for discussion.

Some students with excellent cognitive processing skills, who have a particular aptitude for and acquire an interest in reading, tend to develop advanced reading comprehension skills independently. However, for the majority of students, the strategies they need to develop and demonstrate comprehension need to be made explicit and carefully guided, not just tested, which is the rationale behind this series of books.

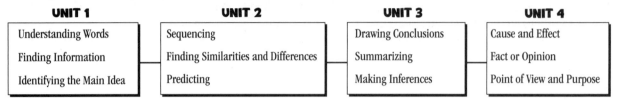

The following twelve comprehension skills are included in this book. Strategies for improving these skills are provided through sets of lessons for each of the skills. These twelve skills have been divided into four units, each with teachers' notes and answer keys, three different comprehension skills, and three student assessment tests.

UNIT 1	UNIT 2	UNIT 3	UNIT 4
Understanding Words	Sequencing	Drawing Conclusions	Cause and Effect
Finding Information	Finding Similarities and Differences	Summarizing	Fact or Opinion
Identifying the Main Idea	Predicting	Making Inferences	Point of View and Purpose

Each skill listed above has a six-page lesson to help students build stronger comprehension skills in that area by using specific strategies.

- Text 1 (first reading text page for use with practice pages)
- Learning Page (learning about the skill with teacher modeling)
- Practice Page (student practice with teacher assistance)
- On Your Own (independent student activity)
- Text 2 (second reading text page for use with practice page)
- Try It Out (independent student activity with one clue)

Text Types

A test at the end of each unit assesses the three skills taught in the unit. The assessment section includes:

- Assessment Text (reading text used for all three assessments)
- Assessment test for the first skill in the unit
- Assessment test for the second skill in the unit
- Assessment test for the third skill in the unit

 Included in this book is a CD containing reproducible, PDF-formatted files for all activity pages, as well as Common Core State Standards. The PDF files are ideal for group instruction using interactive whiteboards.

In addition to applying comprehension strategies to better understand content, students will experience reading and interpreting a variety of text types:

- Reports
- Narratives
- Expositions
- Recounts
- Procedures
- Explanations

Teacher and Student Pages

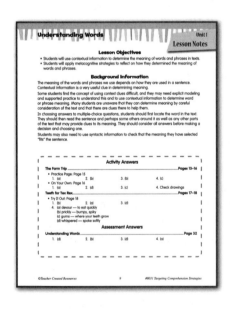

Lesson Notes

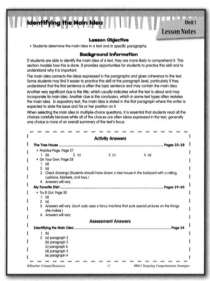

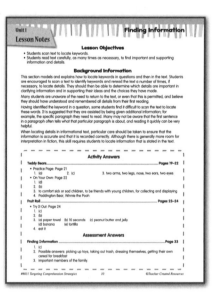

Each of the four units contains lessons that address three specific comprehension skills. Every Lesson Notes page includes:

- Lesson objective indicators state expected outcomes.

- Background information about the skill and teaching strategies.

- An answer key for student pages and assessment pages. (*Note:* Answers may vary, particularly with higher-order comprehension skills. Teachers may choose to accept alternative answers if students are able to justify their responses.)

Helpful Hints

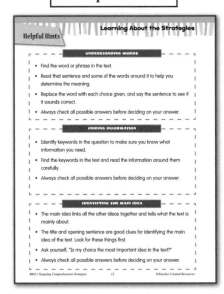

- All three comprehension skills for the unit are identified. These serve as reminders for students as they complete the activities.
- Helpful hints are provided for each skill in bullet-point form.

Text 1

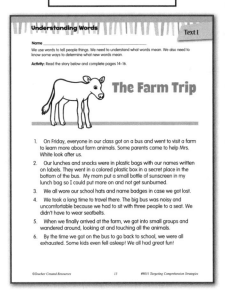

- The skill is identified and defined.
- The text is presented to students using oral, silent, partner, or read-aloud methods. Choose a technique or approach most suitable to your classroom needs.

Learning Page

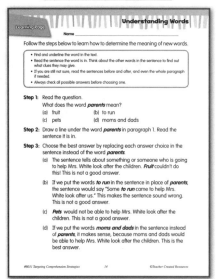

- This is a teacher-student interaction page.
- Steps and strategies are outlined, discussed, and referenced using the text page.
- A multiple-choice question is presented, and metacognitive processes for choosing the best answer are described.

Practice Page

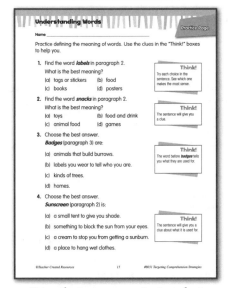

- Using the text page content, students practice strategies to complete the questions. The teacher provides guidance as needed.
- Some multiple-choice questions and others requiring explanations are presented with prompts or clues to assist students.

On Your Own

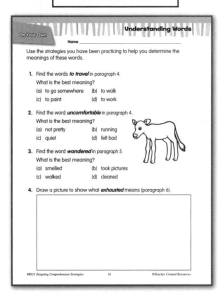

- This page is completed independently.
- At least one multiple-choice question and others requiring explanations are presented for students to complete.

Text 2

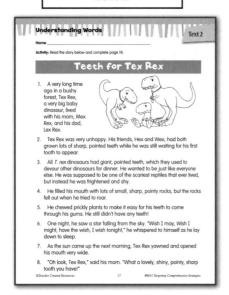

- As with the first text page for the lesson, the skill is identified.

- Presentation of the text is decided by the teacher.

Try It Out

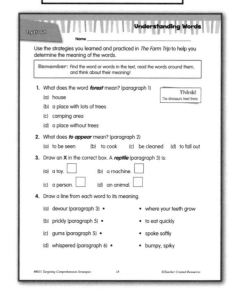

- This page can be completed independently by the student.

- Multiple-choice questions and some requiring explanation are included.

Assessment Text

- The three skills to be tested are identified.

- The assessment text is presented.

Unit Assessments

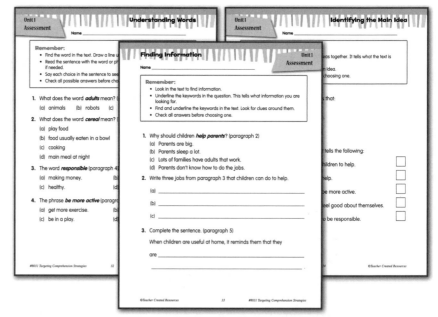

- An assessment page is provided for each of the three skills in the unit.

- The comprehension skill to be tested is identified, and students apply their knowledge and strategies to complete each page, using the content of the Assessment Text page.

- Multiple-choice questions and others requiring more explanation are presented.

Common Core State Standards Correlations

Each lesson meets one or more of the following Common Core State Standards © Copyright 2010. National Governors Association Center for Best Practices and Council of Chief State School Officers. All rights reserved. For more information about the Common Core State Standards, go to *http://www.corestandards.org/* or *http://www.teachercreated.com/standards*.

Reading: Literature Standards	Pages
Key Ideas and Details	
ELA.RL.2.1: Ask and answer such questions as *who, what, where, when, why*, and *how* to demonstrate understanding of key details in a text.	13–16, 17–18, 25–28, 29–30, 39–42, 49–50, 51–54, 55–56, 57–60, 65–68,69–70, 77–80, 81–82, 91–94, 95–96, 107–108, 109–112
ELA.RL.2.2: Recount stories, including fables and folktales from diverse cultures, and determine their central message, lesson, or moral.	25–28, 29–30, 51–54, 55–56, 57–60, 65–68, 77–80, 95–96, 107–108, 109–112
ELA.RL.2.3: Describe how characters in a story respond to major events and challenges.	25–28, 29–30, 51–54, 55–56, 57–60, 65–68, 77–80, 107–108, 109–112
Craft and Structure	
ELA.RL.2.4: Describe how words and phrases (e.g., regular beats, alliteration, rhymes, repeated lines) supply rhythm and meaning in a story, poem, or song.	39–42, 69–70, 91–94, 107–108
ELA.RL.2.5: Describe the overall structure of a story, including describing how the beginning introduces the story and the ending concludes the action.	25–28, 29–30, 39–42, 49–50, 57–60, 65–68, 95–96, 107–108, 109–112
ELA.RL.2.6: Acknowledge differences in the points of view of characters, including by speaking in a different voice for each character when reading dialogue aloud.	107–108
Integration of Knowledge and Ideas	
ELA.RL.2.7: Use information gained from the illustrations and words in a print or digital text to demonstrate understanding of its characters, setting, or plot.	25–28, 29–30, 55–56, 65–68, 95–96
Range of Reading and Level of Text Complexity	
ELA.RL.2.10: By the end of the year, read and comprehend literature, including stories and poetry, in the grades 2–3 text complexity band proficiently, with scaffolding as needed at the high end of the range.	All informational passages allow students to read and comprehend informational texts in the grades 2–3 text complexity band.

Reading: Informational Text Standards	Pages
Key Ideas and Details	
ELA.RI.2.1: Ask and answer such questions as *who, what, where, when, why*, and *how* to demonstrate understanding of key details in a text.	19–22, 23–24, 31–34, 43–44, 45–48, 71–74, 75–76, 83–86, 97–100, 101–102, 103–106
ELA.RI.2.2: Identify the main topic of a multiparagraph text as well as the focus of specific paragraphs within the text.	31–34, 71–74, 75–76, 97–100, 101–102, 103–106
ELA.RI.2.3: Describe the connection between a series of historical events, scientific ideas or concepts, or steps in technical procedures in a text.	23–24, 43–44, 45–48, 83–86
Craft and Structure	
ELA.RI.2.4: Determine the meaning of words and phrases in a text relevant to a grade 2 topic or subject area.	19–22, 23–24, 31–34, 45–48, 71–74, 83–86, 97–100, 101–102, 103–106
ELA.RI.2.5: Know and use various text features (e.g., captions, bold print, subheadings, glossaries, indexes, electronic menus, icons) to locate key facts or information in a text efficiently.	19–22, 23–24, 45–48, 83–86, 97–100, 101–102
ELA.RI.2.6: Identify the main purpose of a text, including what the author wants to answer, explain, or describe.	19–22, 23–24, 31–34, 43–44, 71–74, 75–76, 83–86, 97–100, 101–102, 103–106
Integration of Knowledge and Ideas	
ELA.RI.2.7: Explain how specific images (e.g., a diagram showing how a machine works) contribute to and clarify a text.	19–22, 23–24, 45–48
ELA.RI.2.8: Describe how reasons support specific points the author makes in a text.	19–22, 31–34, 71–74, 75–76, 97–100, 101–102. 103–106
Range of Reading and Level of Text Complexity	
ELA.RI.2.10: By the end of year, read and comprehend informational texts, including history/social studies, science, and technical texts, in the grades 2–3 text complexity band proficiently, with scaffolding as needed at the high end of the range.	All informational passages allow students to read and comprehend informational texts in the grades 2–3 text complexity band.

Lesson Objectives

- Students will use contextual information to determine the meaning of words and phrases in texts.
- Students will apply metacognitive strategies to reflect on how they determined the meaning of words and phrases.

Background Information

The meaning of the words and phrases we use depends on how they are used in a sentence. Contextual information is a very useful clue in determining meaning.

Some students find the concept of using context clues difficult, and they may need explicit modeling and supported practice on how to use contextual information to determine word or phrase meaning. Many students are unaware that they can determine meaning by careful consideration of the text and that there are clues there to help them.

In choosing answers to multiple-choice questions, students should first locate the word in the text. They should then read the sentence, and perhaps some others around it, as well as any other parts of the text that may provide clues to its meaning. They should consider all answers before making a decision and choosing one.

Students may also need to use syntactic information to check that the meaning they have selected "fits" the sentence.

Activity Answers

The Farm Trip ....Pages 13–16

- Practice Page: Page 15
  1. (a)
  2. (b)
  3. (b)
  4. (c)
- On Your Own: Page 16
  1. (a)
  2. (d)
  3. (c)
  4. Drawings will vary. Check for accurancy.

Teeth for Tex Rex...Pages 17–18

- Try It Out: Page 18
  1. (b)
  2. (a)
  3. (d)
  4. (a) devour — to eat quickly
     (b) prickly — bumpy, spiky
     (c) gums — where your teeth grow
     (d) whispered — spoke softly

Assessment Answers

Understanding Words ....Page 32

1. (d)	2. (b)	3. (d)	4. (a)

Lesson Objectives

- Students will scan text to locate keywords.
- Students will read text carefully, as many times as necessary, to find important and supporting information and details.

Background Information

This section models and explains how to locate keywords in questions and then in the text. Students are encouraged to scan a text to identify keywords and reread the text a number of times, if necessary, to locate details. They should then be able to determine which details are important in clarifying information and in supporting their ideas and the choices they have made.

Many students are unaware of the need to return to the text, or even that this is permitted, and believe they should have understood and remembered all details from their first reading.

Having identified the keyword in a question, some students find it difficult to scan the text to locate these words. It is suggested that they are assisted by being given additional information; for example, the specific paragraph they need to read. Many may not be aware that the first sentence in a paragraph often tells what that particular paragraph is about, and reading it quickly can be very helpful.

When locating details in informational text, particular care should be taken to ensure that the information is accurate and that it is recorded correctly. Although there is generally more room for interpretation in fiction, this skill requires students to locate information that is stated in the text.

Activity Answers

Teddy Bears .... **Pages 19–22**

- Practice Page: Page 21
  1. (a)   2. (c)   3. two arms, two legs, nose, two ears, two eyes
- On Your Own: Page 22
  1. (d)
  2. (b)
  3. to comfort sick or sad children, to be friends with young children, for collecting and displaying
  4. Paddington Bear, Winnie the Pooh

Fruit Roll .... **Pages 23–24**

- Try It Out: Page 24
  1. (c)
  2. (b)
  3. (a) paper towel   (b) 10 seconds   (c) peanut butter and jelly
     (d) banana   (e) tortilla
  4. eat it

Assessment Answers

Finding Information .... **Page 33**

  1. (c)
  2. Possible answers: picking up toys, taking out trash, dressing themselves, getting their own cereal for breakfast
  3. important members of the family

Lesson Objective

- Students will determine the main idea in a text and in specific paragraphs.

Background Information

If students are able to identify the main idea of a text, they are more likely to comprehend it. This section models how this is done. It provides opportunities for students to practice this skill and to understand why it is important.

The main idea connects the ideas expressed in the paragraphs and gives coherence to the text. Some students may find it easier to practice this skill at the paragraph level, particularly if they understand that the first sentence is often the topic sentence and may contain the main idea.

Another very significant clue is the title, which usually indicates what the text is about and may incorporate its main idea. Another clue is the conclusion, which in some text types often restates the main idea. In expository text, the main idea is stated in the first paragraph, where the writer is expected to state the issue and his or her position on it.

When selecting the main idea in multiple-choice questions, it is essential that students read all the choices carefully, because while all of the choices are often ideas expressed in the text, generally one choice is more of an overall summary of the text's focus.

Activity Answers

The Tree House .... Pages 25–28

- Practice Page: Page 27
  1. (b)   2. (c)   3. (c)   4. (a)
- On Your Own: Page 28
  1. (d)
  2. (a)
  3. Drawings will vary. (Students should have drawn a tree house with a railing, cushions, blankets, and toys.)
  4. Answers will vary.

My Favorite Shirt .... Pages 29–30

- Try It Out: Page 30
  1. (d)
  2. (a)
  3. Answers will vary. (Aunt Judy uses a fancy machine that puts special pictures on the things she makes.)
  4. Answers will vary.

Assessment Answers

Identifying the Main Idea .... Page 34

1. (b)
2. (a) paragraph 2
   (b) paragraph 3
   (c) paragraph 6
   (d) paragraph 5
   (e) paragraph 4

Helpful Hints

UNDERSTANDING WORDS

- Find the word or phrase in the text.

- Read that sentence and some of the words around it to help you determine the meaning.

- Replace the word with each choice given, and say the sentence aloud to see if it sounds correct.

- Always check all possible answers before deciding on your answer.

FINDING INFORMATION

- Identify keywords in the question to make sure you know what information you need.

- Find the keywords in the text and read the information around them carefully.

- Always check all possible answers before deciding on your answer.

IDENTIFYING THE MAIN IDEA

- The main idea links all the other ideas together and tells what the text is mainly about.

- The title and opening sentence are good clues for identifying the main idea of the text. Look for these things first.

- Ask yourself, "Is my choice the most important idea in the text?"

- Always check all possible answers before deciding on your answer.

Name _____

We use words to tell people things. We need to understand what words mean. We also need to know some ways to determine what new words mean.

Activity: Read the story below and complete pages 14–16.

The Farm Trip

1. On Friday, everyone in our class got on a bus and went to visit a farm to learn more about farm animals. Some parents came to help Mrs. White look after us.

2. Our lunches and snacks were in plastic bags with our names written on labels. They went in a colored plastic box in a secret place in the bottom of the bus. My mom put a small bottle of sunscreen in my lunch bag so I could put more on and not get sunburned.

3. We all wore our school hats and name badges in case we got lost.

4. We took a long time to travel there. The big bus was noisy and uncomfortable because we had to sit with three people to a seat. We didn't have to wear seatbelts.

5. When we finally arrived at the farm, we got into small groups and wandered around, looking at and touching all the animals.

6. By the time we got on the bus to go back to school, we were all exhausted. Some kids even fell asleep! We all had great fun!

Name _____

Follow the steps below to learn how to determine the meaning of new words.

- Find and underline the word in the text.
- Read the sentence the word is in. Think about the other words in the sentence to find out what clues they may give.
- If you are still not sure, read the sentences before and after, and even the whole paragraph if needed.
- Always check all possible answers before choosing one.

Step 1: Read the question.

What does the word *parents* mean?

(a) fruit   (b) to run

(c) pets   (d) moms and dads

Step 2: Draw a line under the word *parents* in paragraph 1. Read the sentence it is in.

Step 3: Choose the best answer by replacing each answer choice in the sentence instead of the word *parents*.

(a) The sentence tells about something or someone who is going to help Mrs. White look after the children. *Fruit* couldn't do this! This is not a good answer.

(b) If we put the words *to run* in the sentence in place of *parents*, the sentence would say "Some *to run* came to help Mrs. White look after us." This makes the sentence sound wrong. This is not a good answer.

(c) *Pets* would not be able to help Mrs. White look after the children. This is not a good answer.

(d) If we put the words *moms and dads* in the sentence instead of *parents*, it makes sense, because moms and dads would be able to help Mrs. White look after the children. This is the best answer.

Understanding Words

Name _____

Practice defining the meaning of words. Use the clues in the "Think!" boxes to help you.

1. Find the word *labels* in paragraph 2.
   What is the best meaning?

   (a) tags or stickers   (b) food

   (c) books   (d) posters

   > **Think!**
   > Try each choice in the sentence. See which one makes the most sense.

2. Find the word *snacks* in paragraph 2.
   What is the best meaning?

   (a) toys   (b) food and drink

   (c) animal food   (d) games

   > **Think!**
   > The sentence will give you a clue.

3. Choose the best answer.

   Badges (paragraph 3) are:

   (a) animals that build burrows.

   (b) labels you wear to tell who you are.

   (c) kinds of trees.

   (d) homes.

   > **Think!**
   > The word before *badges* tells you what they are used for.

4. Choose the best answer.

   Sunscreen (paragraph 2) is:

   (a) a small tent to give you shade.

   (b) something to block the sun from your eyes.

   (c) a cream to stop you from getting a sunburn.

   (d) a place to hang wet clothes.

   > **Think!**
   > The sentence will give you a clue about what it is used for.

Name _____

Use the strategies you have been practicing to help you determine the meanings of these words.

1. Find the words *to travel* in paragraph 4.

What is the best meaning?

(a) to go somewhere   (b) to walk

(c) to paint   (d) to work

2. Find the word *uncomfortable* in paragraph 4.

What is the best meaning?

(a) not pretty   (b) running

(c) quiet   (d) felt bad

3. Find the word *wandered* in paragraph 5.

What is the best meaning?

(a) smelled   (b) took pictures

(c) walked   (d) cleaned

4. Draw a picture to show what *exhausted* means (paragraph 6).

Name _____

Activity: Read the story below and complete page 18.

Teeth for Tex Rex

1.   A very long time ago in a bushy forest, Tex Rex, a very big baby dinosaur, lived with his mom, Mex Rex, and his dad, Lex Rex.

2.   Tex Rex was very unhappy. His friends, Hex and Wex, had both grown lots of sharp, pointed teeth while he was still waiting for his first tooth to appear.

3.   All *T. rex* dinosaurs had giant, pointed teeth, which they used to devour other dinosaurs for dinner. He wanted to be just like everyone else. He was supposed to be one of the scariest reptiles that ever lived, but instead he was frightened and shy.

4.   He filled his mouth with lots of small, sharp, pointy rocks, but the rocks fell out when he tried to roar.

5.   He chewed prickly plants to make it easy for his teeth to come through his gums. He still didn't have any teeth!

6.   One night, he saw a star falling from the sky. "Wish I may, Wish I might, have the wish, I wish tonight," he whispered to himself as he lay down to sleep.

7.   As the sun came up the next morning, Tex Rex yawned and opened his mouth very wide.

8.   "Oh look, Tex Rex," said his mom. "What a lovely, shiny, pointy, sharp tooth you have!"

Name _____

Use the strategies you learned and practiced in *The Farm Trip* to help you determine the meaning of the words.

> **Remember:** Find the word or words in the text, read the words around them, and think about their meaning!

1. What does the word **forest** mean? (paragraph 1)

> **Think!**
> The dinosaurs lived there.

(a) house

(b) a place with lots of trees

(c) camping area

(d) a place without trees

2. What does **to appear** mean? (paragraph 2)

(a) to be seen   (b) to cook   (c) be cleaned   (d) to fall out

3. Draw an **X** in the correct box. A **reptile** (paragraph 3) is:

(a) a toy. ☐   (b) a machine. ☐

(c) a person. ☐   (d) an animal. ☐

4. Draw a line from each word to its meaning.

(a) devour (paragraph 3) •   • where your teeth grow

(b) prickly (paragraph 5) •   • to eat quickly

(c) gums (paragraph 5) •   • spoke softly

(d) whispered (paragraph 6) •   • bumpy, spiky

Name _____

When you read, you can usually remember some of the things you have read. If you are asked questions, you should reread the text to find information and check that you are correct. The answer is there, so you just need to find it!

Activity: Read the passage below and complete pages 20–22.

Teddy Bears

1. Teddy bears are stuffed toy bears.

2. Teddy bears have soft fur on their bodies. They have two arms and two legs. They have a big, black, squashed nose and two small, round ears that stand up. They usually have big, brown eyes.

3. Teddy bears can help sick or sad children feel better. They make good friends for young children.

4. Teddy bears come in different sizes and colors. Many are dressed in cute costumes.

5. Teddy bears were named after an American president named Theodore Roosevelt. His nickname was "Teddy."

6. Some adults like to collect teddy bears to display. Some of these teddy bears can be very expensive.

7. Two well-known teddy bears in stories are Paddington Bear and Winnie the Pooh.

8. Teddy bears are great toys for anyone to own.

Name _____

Follow the steps below to learn how to find information in the text.

> • Read the question very carefully. Keywords will tell you what information and details you need to find.
> • Underline the keywords in the question.
> • Think about an answer, but you should look at the text again to check that you are correct.
> • Find the keywords in the text. Carefully read the information around them.
> • Check all the answers before choosing one.

Step 1: Read the question.

What are teddy bears?

(a) Teddy bears are wind-up toys.

(b) Teddy bears are real animals.

(c) Teddy bears are stuffed toy bears.

(d) Teddy bears are plants.

Step 2: The keywords are *what* and *teddy bears.* Underline them in the question.

Step 3: Choose the best answer by thinking about each choice carefully.

(a) Teddy bears are toys but not wind-up toys. This is not the best answer.

(b) Teddy bears are toys and are not real. This is not a good answer.

(c) The first sentence in the text says that teddy bears are stuffed toy bears. This is the best answer.

(d) Teddy bears are not plants. This is not a good answer.

Name _____

Practice finding information. Use the clues in the "Think!" boxes to help you.

1. What are the bodies of teddy bears covered with?

   (a) Teddy bears have soft fur.

   (b) Teddy bears have scales.

   (c) Teddy bears have hair.

   (d) Teddy bears have spikes.

   > **Think!**
   > Find the exact words in paragraph 2.

2. Where did the name "teddy bear" come from?

   (a) Teddy bears are named after a town.

   (b) Teddy bears are named after Mr. Ted.

   (c) Teddy bears are named after a man whose nickname was "Teddy."

   (d) Teddy bears are named after a bear in a book.

   > **Think!**
   > Read paragraph 5.

3. Write a list of body parts that all teddy bears should have.

   > **Think!**
   > Find a paragraph that lists all the body parts.

   - _____

   - _____

   - _____

   - _____

   - _____

Name _____

Use the strategies you have been practicing to help you find information in the text.

1. What color are teddy bears' noses? (paragraph 2)

   (a) red   (b) blue

   (c) brown   (d) black

2. What can be different about teddy bears? (paragraph 4)

   (a) the number of arms and legs

   (b) their size and color

   (c) the number of noses

   (d) the number of eyes

3. Write two things that teddy bears are used for. (paragraphs 3 and 6)

   • _____

   _____

   • _____

   _____

4. Write the names of two well-known teddy bears. (paragraph 7)

Name _____

Activity: Read the recipe below and complete page 24.

• • • • • FRUIT ROLL • • • • •

You will need:

- 1 small flour tortilla
- 2 teaspoons of peanut butter
- 2 teaspoons of jelly
- paper towel
- teaspoon

- 1 peeled banana
- knife
- microwave oven

Steps:

(a) Put the tortilla on a paper towel.

(b) Microwave it for 10 seconds.

(c) Spread peanut butter on the tortilla.

(d) Spread jelly on top.

(e) Put the banana near the edge of the tortilla.

(f) Roll up the tortilla.

Test:

Eat and enjoy!

Try It Out

Name _____

Use the strategies you learned and practiced in *Teddy Bears* to help you find information.

Remember:

- Find the keywords in the questions and in the text.
- Check all answers before choosing one.

1. How many *things* do you need to make fruit rolls?

    (a) 4   (b) 6   (c) 8   (d) 5

Think!

Count everything you need! Not just the ingredients!

2. What two spreads are used?

    (a) honey and jelly

    (b) peanut butter and jelly

    (c) peanut butter and honey

    (d) honey and cheese

3. Complete the sentences about the *steps*.

    (a) The tortilla is placed on a _____.

    (b) The tortilla is microwaved for _____.

    (c) The tortilla is spread with _____

        and _____.

    (d) The _____ is placed near the
        edge of the tortilla.

    (e) Roll up the _____.

4. How can you *test* the recipe? _____

Name _____

If you know the main idea of a text, you will have a much better chance of understanding what the content is about.

Activity: Read the story below and complete pages 26–28.

The Tree House

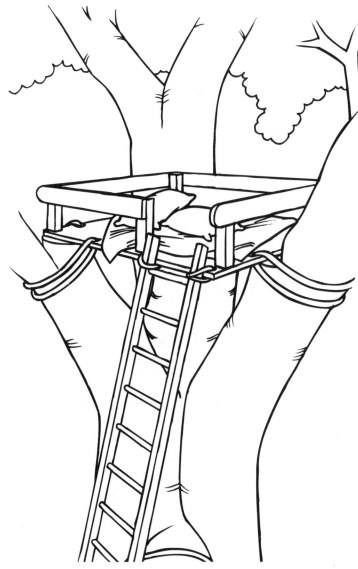

1.   This is how we built a tree house in the big tree in our backyard.

2.   Mom and Dad helped us build it with scraps of wood and junk. We found lots of junk in the shed we could use.

3.   We tied rope to an old ladder. Then, we tied the ladder to the trunk of the tree.

4.   We used a big, flat piece of wood for a floor in the fork of the tree. Then, we used more rope and nails to fix the floor to the tree.

5.   We made a railing around the sides to stop us from falling out. We used bits of an old fence.

6.   Finally, we placed soft cushions and blankets in the tree house for us to sit on.

7.   Mark, Karl, Kim, and I had great fun building and playing in our tree house. Even our toys had fun!

Name _____

Follow the steps below to learn how to determine the main idea and why it is important.

> - There are often many ideas in a text, but there is only one idea that joins the other ideas together. This is the main idea.
> - Read the text, and then ask yourself, "What is it mainly about?" (The title is a very good clue to the main idea because a good title often tells the reader what the text is about.)
> - Always check all the answers before choosing one.

Step 1: Read what you need to find out.

The main idea of *The Tree House* is:

(a)   about a book.

(b)   about a family.

(c)   how nice trees look in the backyard.

(d)   how a tree house can be made.

Step 2: Choose the best answer by thinking about each choice carefully. Look for the choice that best describes the text.

(a)   The text is not about books. This is not a good answer.

(b)   The names of some people are given in the text. This is a little idea but not the main idea. This is not the best answer.

(c)   The text tells about trees and backyards but only a little bit. The text does not tell how nice trees look in the backyard. This is not a good answer.

(d)   The text gives lots of steps to explain how a tree house was made. This is the best answer.

Identifying the Main Idea

Name _____

Practice finding the main idea. Use the clues in the "Think!" boxes to help you.

1. Paragraph 1 is mainly about:

   (a) playing in the backyard.

   (b) where the tree house was built.

   (c) trees are homes for birds.

   (d) plants are nice to look at.

> **Think!**
> Read paragraph 1 a few times. What do the words tell about?

2. Which paragraph tells what they used to get up into the tree?

   (a) paragraph 1   (b) paragraph 2

   (c) paragraph 3   (d) paragraph 4

> **Think!**
> Look for the name of something that is used for climbing.

3. What is the main idea of paragraph 2?

   (a) Dinner is ready.

   (b) Mom and Dad are good parents.

   (c) Finding junk material for the tree house

   (d) The tree house is cozy.

> **Think!**
> Think about the answers then read the paragraph again.

4. Which paragraph tells how to put a *floor* in the tree house?

   (a) paragraph 4   (b) paragraph 6

   (c) paragraph 5   (d) paragraph 2

> **Think!**
> Look for the word *floor*.

Name _____

Use the strategies your have been practicing to help you identify the main idea.

1. What is the main idea of paragraph 6?

   (a) Having a tree house is fun.

   (b) Tree homes can be big.

   (c) A lot of people can fit in a tree house.

   (d) We made the tree house comfortable.

2. What is the main idea of paragraph 5?

   (a) The tree house had a railing to keep the children safe.

   (b) Fences are useful.

   (c) Trains go on railway tracks.

   (d) The tree house had a roof.

3. Draw a tree house in a backyard. Put the three main ideas from paragraphs 5, 6, and 7 in your drawing.

4. Titles help to tell about the main idea of a text. Is the title *The Tree House* a good clue? Choose *Yes* or *No*.

Yes	No

Name _____

Activity: Read the story below and complete page 30.

My Favorite Shirt

1. Aunt Judy made me a light blue shirt for my birthday last year.

2. My blue shirt has long sleeves and a high neck. The cuffs and collar are dark blue. Blue is my favorite color. It matches my dark blue track pants.

3. We live in a place where it is very cold in the winter. Sometimes it snows. We need to wear lots of clothes to keep warm. The blue shirt is made from thick, fluffy material. It helps me to keep warm.

4. Aunt Judy sews very well. She is always making something for someone. Everyone likes to get something made by Aunt Judy. She makes each thing different and special.

5. Uncle Frank bought Aunt Judy a fancy sewing machine. The sewing machine draws pictures on the clothes she makes. I like airplanes, so Aunt Judy sewed a colored airplane on my shirt.

6. I love wearing my favorite blue shirt. I wonder what Aunt Judy will make for me next year.

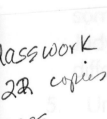

classwork
22 copies
pages
25, 26, 27, 28

Name _____

Use the strategies you learned and practiced in *The Tree House* to help you identify the main ideas.

Remember:

- The information is usually in the text.
- Ask yourself, "Which answer tells what the paragraph/text is mainly about?"
- Look at the title, too!
- Read all the answers carefully before deciding.

---

1. What is the main idea of paragraph 3?

    (a) The shirt keeps the writer cool.

    (b) The shirt is pretty.

    (c) The shirt was a birthday present.

    (d) The shirt keeps the writer warm.

> **Think!**
> Make sure that you are looking in paragraph 3.

2. What is the main idea of paragraph 4?

    (a) Everyone likes what Aunt Judy makes them because she sews very well.

    (b) Aunt Judy does not sew well.

    (c) Aunt Judy only sews winter clothes.

    (d) Aunt Judy makes all her own clothes.

3. Write a sentence to tell the main idea of paragraph 5.

    _____

    _____

4. Choose *Yes* or *No*.
    The title tells the main idea of the whole text.

Yes	No

Name _____

Activity: Read the passage below, and use pages 32–34 to show how well you can understand words, find information, and identify main ideas.

HELPING AT HOME

1. Doing jobs at home is good for children. I think all children should have some jobs to do at home.

2. Parents are very busy. In lots of families, the adults work outside of the home. Children can help by doing jobs around the house. This helps everyone in the family.

3. Children are little, but they can help by picking up their toys, taking out the trash, dressing themselves, and getting their own cereal for breakfast. This helps because adults don't have to do them as well as the bigger jobs they have to do.

4. Doing jobs at home teaches children to be responsible. They learn to take charge of the things they have to do. Doing jobs helps children grow up to be responsible adults.

5. When children do jobs to help, they are being useful. It reminds them that they are important members of the family. It makes them feel good about themselves.

6. Doing jobs can be fun and good exercise, too! When children are putting away toys or helping wash the car, they are exercising. Doing jobs helps children be more active.

7. Doing jobs at home is good for everyone. I think all children should help out at home.

Name _____

> **Remember:**
> - Find the word in the text. Draw a line under it.
> - Read the sentence with the word or phrase in it and the ones around it if needed.
> - Say each choice in the sentence to see which one makes the most sense.
> - Check all possible answers before choosing one.

1. What does the word **_adults_** mean? (paragraph 3)

(a) animals   (b) robots   (c) friends   (d) grown-ups

2. What does the word **_cereal_** mean? (paragraph 3)

(a) play food

(b) food usually eaten in a bowl

(c) cooking

(d) main meal at night

3. The word **_responsible_** (paragraph 4) means:

(a) making money.   (b) clean.

(c) healthy.   (d) be in charge of.

4. The phrase **_be more active_** (paragraph 6) means:

(a) get more exercise.   (b) be busy.

(c) be in a play.   (d) grow.

Name _____

Remember:

- Look in the text to find information.
- Underline the keywords in the question. This tells what information you are looking for.
- Find and underline the keywords in the text. Look for clues around them.
- Check all answers before choosing one.

---

1. Why should children *help parents*? (paragraph 2)

    (a) Parents need more exercise.

    (b) Parents sleep a lot.

    (c) Lots of families have adults that work.

    (d) Parents don't know how to do the jobs.

2. Write three jobs from paragraph 3 that children can do to help.

    - _____

    - _____

    - _____

3. Complete the sentence. (paragraph 5)

    When children are useful at home, it reminds them that they

    are _____

    _____ .

Name _____

Remember:
- The main idea joins all the other ideas together. It tells what the text is mainly about.
- The title gives a clue about the main idea.
- Check all possible answers before choosing one.

---

1. The main idea of the whole text is that:

   (a) children are clever.

   (b) children should help at home.

   (c) children are busy people.

   (d) children are always naughty.

2. Write the paragraph number that tells the following:

   (a) Parents are busy and need children to help. ☐

   (b) Children can do little jobs to help. ☐

   (c) Doing jobs helps children to be more active. ☐

   (d) Doing jobs helps children to feel good about themselves. ☐

   (e) Doing jobs teaches children to be responsible. ☐

Lesson Objective

- Students will sequence events.

Background Information

This section demonstrates how to determine the order in which events occur, sometimes using time markers and other strategies to identify the relationship between events.

Knowing the sequence of events is an important and often critical factor in a reader's understanding of a text.

First, students need to determine from the question which events they are required to sequence. Then, they should locate them in the text and look for any time-marker words that could be helpful. Examples could include: *before, then, when, while, after, finally, at last,* or *following.*

Students may also find creating timelines of sections of the text or specific events a useful strategy.

Activity Answers

I Jump Out of Bed .... **Pages 39–42**

- Practice Page: Page 41
  1. (b)
  2. (c)
  3. (c)
  4. (d)
- On Your Own: Page 42
  1. (a)
  2. (b)
  3. (a) 8   (b) 6   (c) 4   (d) 2
     (e) 3   (f) 1   (g) 5   (h) 7
  4. Answers will vary.

How to Make Fairy Bread .... **Pages 43–44**

- Try It Out: Page 44
  1. (d)
  2. (b)
  3. (a) Use the knife to butter the slices of bread.
     (b) Cut the fairy bread into triangles.

Assessment Answers

Sequencing .... **Page 58**

  1. (d)
  2. (b)
  3. 3, 4, 1, 2

Lesson Objective

- Students will compare and contrast people, places, and events.

Background Information

The ability to compare and contrast the information provided in a text enhances the reader's understanding of that text and is an important comprehension skill students need to practice.

Students are required to categorize information in order to determine what some people, places, and events have in common or how they differ.

Graphic organizers are very useful tools for identifying similarities and differences, particularly Venn diagrams, T–charts, and compare-and-contrast charts.

same	different

T-chart

A	B	A	B
compare		contrast	

Compare-and-Contrast chart

Activity Answers

My Family .... **Pages 45–48**

- Practice Page: Page 47
    1. (a)   2. (b)   3. (c)   4. (d)
    5. Mom and "me"
- On Your Own: Page 48
    1. (b)
    2. (d)
    3. (a) True   (b) False   (c) False   (d) True   (e) False
    4. Dad — make things
       Mom — walk/garden
       "me" — do puzzles
       Gran — go to gym/bowl/go on bus trips
       Steve — boss younger sister

My Favorite Places .... **Pages 49–50**

- Try It Out: Page 50
    1. (c)
    2. (c)
    3. Drawings will vary.
    4. Answers will vary.

Assessment Answers

Finding Similarities and Differences...**Page 59**

1. (c)
2.

	Morning	Lunch	Afternoon
Bill and Bob			✓
Mrs. Stout	✓		
Mrs. Snoop		✓	
Mr. Cream	✓		

3. (b)

Lesson Objective

- Students will use information from a text to predict outcomes not explicitly stated in the text.

Background Information

To be able to predict outcomes, often in terms of the probable actions or reactions of specific characters, students need to focus on content and understand what they read. They need to monitor their understanding as they read, constantly confirming, rejecting, or adjusting their predictions.

The focus of this section is on teaching students how to locate and use the information provided in the text to determine probable outcomes and then to evaluate their predictions.

Students need to be able to locate specific information related to an issue and/or characters, using keywords and concepts. Their predictions should not be wild guesses, but well thought-out, relevant ideas based on the information provided and some prior knowledge.

If students' answers differ, it is suggested that they check again to see why their answer varies from the one given. If they can justify their answer, teachers may decide to accept it.

Activity Answers

The Man and the Singing Bird ....**Pages 51–54**

- Practice Page: Page 53
  1. (b)
  2. Drawings will vary.
  3. (a)
- On Your Own: Page 54
  1. (d)
  2. (c)
  3. Drawings will vary.

The Lion and the Dolphin .... **Pages 55–56**

- Try It Out: Page 56
  1. (c)
  2. All answers may be acceptable as long as students can justify their answers.
  3. Drawings will vary.

Assessment Answers

Predicting ....**Page 60**

1. (d)
2. Answers will vary.

Helpful Hints

SEQUENCING

- Make sure you know which events you need to sequence. Then find those events in the text.

- Pay attention to how they are related. Making a mental picture of what is happening in the text sometimes helps you imagine the sequence.

- Always check all possible answers before deciding on your answer.

FINDING SIMILARITIES AND DIFFERENCES

- Make sure you understand the question before you begin. Then find the keywords.

- Use a chart, table, Venn diagram, or other type of organizer, if you need to. This will help you find similarities and differences.

- Always check all possible answers before deciding on your answer.

PREDICTING

- You need to find the information that connects to the question.

- The answer will not be found in the text, but there is information you can use and think about as you read. The writer will suggest, rather than tell, what is likely to happen. You must use the details in the text to help you predict.

- Always check all possible answers before deciding on your answer.

Name _____

Sequence is the order in which events happen. To fully understand what you read, you must pay attention to the sequencing of events.

Activity: Read the poem below and complete pages 40–42.

I Jump Out of Bed

1. First, I jump out of bed in the morning.

   I jump out of bed in the morning.

   I jump out of bed in the morning.

   Then, I make my bed.

2. Next, I eat breakfast in the morning.

   I eat breakfast in the morning.

   I eat breakfast in the morning.

   Then, I rinse my dishes.

3. Then, I brush my teeth in the morning.

   I brush my teeth in the morning.

   I brush my teeth in the morning.

   Then, I get dressed in my school clothes.

4. Then, I pack my school bag in the morning.

   I pack my school bag in the morning.

   I pack my school bag in the morning.

   Finally, I walk to school.

Name _____

Follow the steps below to learn how to determine the sequence of events.

- Order is very important.
- Ask, "Which events need to be sequenced?"
- Find the events in the text and underline them.
- Pay attention to how these events fit together. Look for time-marker words, such as *then, before, next,* etc.
- Check ALL the answers before deciding.

Step 1: Read the question.

What happens *first* in the morning?

(a) I make my bed.   (b) I yawn.

(c) I stretch.   (d) I jump out of bed.

Step 2: The important word in the question is *first.* Underline it.

Step 3: Find the word *first* in the text. Underline it. (*First* is a time-marker word.)

First means the part of the text you are looking for comes before other parts of the text.

Step 4: Choose the best answer by thinking about each choice carefully.

(a) The child does make the bed, but it is not the first thing done. It does not come in the first part of the text. It is the second thing the child does. This is not the best answer.

(b) The text does not tell us that the child yawned. This is not a good answer.

(c) The text does not tell us that the child stretched. This is not a good answer.

(d) "I jump out of bed" comes first in the text and follows the word *First* (a time-marker word). This is the best answer.

Sequencing

Name _____

Practice sequencing the order of events. Use the clues in the "Think!" boxes to help you.

1. What does the child do **after** eating breakfast?

   (a) jump out of bed   (b) rinse the dishes

   (c) clean the kitchen   (d) read a book

   > **Think!**
   > Find "eat breakfast" in the text and see what comes **after** it.

2. What was the **next** thing to happen after the child rinsed the dishes?

   (a) watch television

   (b) go to school

   (c) brush her teeth

   (d) The family had lunch.

   > **Think!**
   > Find the words "Then I rinse my dishes," then read the very **next** event.

3. What does the child do **before** eating breakfast?

   (a) homework   (b) brush her teeth

   (c) make the bed   (d) play a game

   > **Think!**
   > Some of the answers are silly. Read the others carefully and choose.

4. What is the **final** (last) thing that the child does?

   (a) go to sleep

   (b) take a bath

   (c) pack her school bag

   (d) walk to school

   > **Think!**
   > Look for a bigger word with **final** in it. The answer is near the word.

Name _____

Use the strategies you have been practicing to help you determine the sequence of events.

1. What did the child do just **before** getting dressed in her school clothes?

   (a) brush her teeth   (b) rinse the dishes

   (c) walk to school   (d) play with a toy

2. Just **before** the child walked to school, she:

   (a) ate breakfast.   (b) packed her school bag.

   (c) fell asleep.   (d) took a bath.

3. Number the events in the correct story order from 1–8.

   (a) walk to school ☐   (b) get dressed   ☐

   (c) rinse dishes   ☐   (d) make the bed   ☐

   (e) eat breakfast   ☐   (f) jump out of bed ☐

   (g) brush teeth   ☐   (h) pack school bag ☐

4. Write steps in order to tell what you do to get ready for school.

   _____

   _____

   _____

   _____

Name _____

Activity: Read the recipe below and complete page 44.

How to Make Fairy Bread

Fairy bread is easy to make.

Make some for a party or another special time.

You will need:

- a cutting board
- a plate
- a butter knife
- slices of bread
- butter
- colored sprinkles

Steps:

1. First, put the slices of bread on the cutting board.

2. Then, use the knife to butter the slices of bread.

3. Next, shake colored sprinkles onto the buttered bread.

4. Then, have an adult cut the fairy bread into triangles.

5. Finally, place the fairy bread on a plate to serve.

Test:

Eat and enjoy!

Name _____

Use the strategies you learned and practiced in *I Jump Out of Bed* to help you determine the sequence of events.

> **Remember:**
> - Order is very important.
> - Ask, "Which events need to be sequenced?"
> - Find the events in the text and underline them.
> - Pay attention to how these events fit together. Look for time-marker words, like *then, before, next,* etc.
> - Check ALL the answers before deciding.

1. What should you do ***first***?

    (a) Cut up the bread.

    (b) Eat the fairy bread.

    (c) Butter the bread.

    (d) Put the bread on the cutting board.

> **Think!**
> Find the answers in the text. Determine which one comes first.

2. What is the ***last*** (final) step?

    (a) Cut the fairy bread into triangles.

    (b) Place the fairy bread onto a plate to serve.

    (c) Shake on the sprinkles.

    (d) Butter the bread.

3. Write the ***next step after*** each of the ones below.

    (a) Put the slices of bread on the cutting board.

    _____

    (b) Shake colored sprinkles onto the buttered bread.

    _____

Finding Similarities and Differences

Name _____

Finding out how things are similar or different can help you understand what you read.

Activity: Read the table below that tells about a family and complete pages 46–48.

My Family

	Dad	**Mom**	**me**	**Gran**	**Steve**
What they look like	tall black hair brown eyes skinny very fit	tall black hair brown eyes freckles	young short freckles brown eyes brown hair	old short gray hair brown eyes	tall brown eyes black hair
The job they do	cameraman for a television station	sell dresses in a dress shop	go to school help at home	clean house babysit	go to school help at home
What they like to do	read run make things	walk read garden	read play cards run do puzzles	go to gym play cards bowl go on bus trips	boss younger sister run
What they like to wear	jeans and a shirt	nice dresses	shorts and T-shirt	pink tracksuit	tracksuit and running shoes

Finding Similarities and Differences

Name _____

Follow the steps below to learn how to organize information in order to make it easy to answer questions about similarities and differences.

> • What is the question asking for? Underline the keywords.
> • A table or chart can help you to see similarities and differences.
> • Check all answers before deciding.

Step 1: Read the question.

Which three people in the family are tall?

(a) Mom and Dad

(b) Gran and "me"

(c) Gran, Steve, and "me"

(d) Dad, Mom, and Steve

Step 2: Underline the keywords *three* and *tall* in the question. This is the important information to look for about the people. You need to find three people who are tall.

Step 3: Choose the best answer by thinking about each choice carefully.

(a) Dad and Mom are tall. This may be a good answer, but the question asks for three people. There are only two people in this answer choice. This is not a good answer.

(b) Gran and "me" are short. There are also only two people in this choice. The question asks for three tall people. This is not a good answer.

(c) There are three people in this answer so this could be a good answer. In the table, Steve is tall, but Gran is short and so is "me." This is not the best answer.

(d) There are three people in this answer so this could be the best answer, but we need to check in the table. Dad is tall, Mom is tall, and Steve is tall. This is the best answer.

Name _____

Practice finding similarities and differences. Use the clues in the "Think!" boxes to help you.

1. Which three people have black hair?

(a) Dad, Mom, and Steve   (b) Steve and "me"

(c) Gran and Mom   (d) Mom, Gran, and Steve

> **Think!**
> Find answers with three people. Read the table.

2. Which two people are short?

(a) Dad and Steve   (b) Gran and "me"

(c) Mom and Gran   (d) Gran and Steve

> **Think!**
> There are two people in each answer. Look for the word **short** in the table.

3. Who likes to play cards?

(a) Dad   (b) Mom

(c) Gran and "me"   (d) Steve

> **Think!**
> Read the things each person likes to do.

4. Three people like to run. Who are they?

(a) Mom, Steve, and "me"   (b) Dad, Mom, and Gran

(c) Mom, Gran, and Steve   (d) Dad, Steve, and "me"

> **Think!**
> Find the names in the table.

5. Write the names of two people with freckles.

_____ and _____

Name _____

Use the strategies you have been practicing to help you identify similarities and differences.

1. Which three people like to read?

   (a) Steve and "me"   (b) Dad, Mom, and "me"

   (c) Gran and "me"   (d) Dad, Steve, and "me"

2. Which person is different from the others because he/she likes to wear "dressy" clothes?

   (a) Gran   (b) Steve

   (c) Dad   (d) Mom

3. Read each statement. Choose *True* or *False*.

	True	False
(a) Everyone has brown eyes.	True	False
(b) Everyone likes to wear sports clothes.	True	False
(c) Everyone has black hair.	True	False
(d) Everyone likes to exercise.	True	False
(e) The children don't help at home.	True	False

4. Write words in the table to show one thing that each person likes to do that is different from the others.

Dad	Mom	me	Gran	Steve

Name _____

Activity: Read the story below and complete page 50.

My Favorite Places

1.   My backyard and my bedroom are my two favorite places.

2.   In my backyard, I have a tree house, a sandbox, a slide, and a swing set.

3.   I have a little patch of garden where Mom is helping me grow flowers and tomatoes.

4.   I can sit on the grass and feel the warm sun on my face.

5.   I play in this favorite place with Bess, my dog, and Clyde, my cat.

6.   In my bedroom, I have a bed, a closet, and a chest of drawers. I have a bookcase and a big toy box. My toy dog, rabbit, and teddy bear sit on the top.

7.   My bedroom has stars, planets, the sun, the moon, and spaceships on the walls and ceiling. I can lie on my starry blanket and look up at the sun or just daydream.

8.   I play in this favorite place with my cars, trucks, and robots on my rug.

9.   My favorite places are special to me.

Name _____

Use the strategies you learned and practiced in *My Family* to help you recognize similarities and differences.

Remember:
- What is the question asking for? Underline the keywords.
- A table or chart can help you to see similarities and differences.
- Check all answers before deciding.

1. The backyard and the bedroom both have:

   (a) a slide.　　　　(b) a sandbox.

   (c) a sun.　　　　(d) grass.

Think!
Find the choices given in the text. Read where they are.

2. The backyard and the bedroom both have:

   (a) a plant.　　(b) a cat.　　(c) a dog.　　(d) a bed.

3. Draw something in your bedroom that is:

   (a) the same as in this bedroom. *in the story.*　　(b) different from this bedroom.

4. Circle the things that you have in your backyard or at a park where you play.

| tree house | sandbox | slide | dog |
| tomatoes | grass | flowers | cat |

Name _____

As we read, we need to pay attention to what is happening and to think about what may happen next.

Activity: Read the story below and complete pages 52–54.

The Man and the Singing Bird

1.   One night, a man heard a bird singing happily.

2.   The man really liked the singing. He set a trap for the bird by putting food in a cage and leaving the door open.

3.   "I've caught you now," he said. "So you can sing for me all the time!"

4.   "I can't sing in a cage," said the bird.

5.   "If you can't sing for me," said the man, "I will have to eat you on toast."

6.   "No! Please don't eat me!" cried the bird. "Set me free, and I will tell you three important things. These three things will be worth a lot more to you than eating me."

7.   The man set the bird free. He flew up onto a branch of a tree.

8.   Then, the bird said to the man, "These are the three things I have to tell you:

   One—Never believe something a captive bird tells you!

   Two—Keep what you have!

   Three—Don't be sad when you have lost something forever!"

9.   Then, the singing bird flew away.

Name _____

Follow the steps below to learn how to make a prediction about what may happen next.

> • The answers are not in the text.
> • Find information in the text to use and think about.
> • Find and underline information that relates to the question.
> • Think hard! What is the writer suggesting might happen?
> • Think about all answers before deciding.

Step 1: Read the question.

What will the bird probably do now that he is free?

(a) find another man to sing for

(b) eat toast

(c) lay eggs

(d) sing in a new place that is safer

Step 2: Choose the best answer by thinking about each choice carefully.

(a) The bird would probably have been frightened by the man. He was almost eaten. He probably wouldn't find another man to sing for. This is not a good answer.

(b) Birds do eat toast, but this bird was almost put on toast and eaten by the man. Toast might remind him about how he was caught and almost eaten. This may not be the best answer.

(c) The text says "*He* flew up . . . ." This tells us that the bird is not a female bird. Only female birds lay eggs. This is not a good answer.

(d) The bird is a singing bird. He will keep on singing. But he will probably find a new, safer place to sing next time. This is the best answer.

Predicting

Name _____

Practice making predictions. Use the clues in the "Think!" boxes to help you.

1. How will the bird most likely feel next time he sings at night?

   (a) hungry   (b) happy

   (c) tired   (d) sad

> **Think!**
> Read the first sentence and underline the part about the bird singing.

2. Draw a picture of the kind of trap you think the man may use next time.

> **Think!**
> Read how the man caught the bird in the story. Think of how he might do it next time.

3. What would the man most likely have done if he hadn't caught the bird?

   (a) He would keep on trying.

   (b) He would make dinner.

   (c) He would go for a walk.

   (d) He would read a book.

> **Think!**
> Read the first four sentences. Underline the parts that tell about the singing.

Name _____

Use the strategies you have been practicing to help you make predictions.

1. Next time people tell the man that they will do something, what will he most likely do?

    (a) listen carefully

    (b) run away

    (c) eat toast

    (d) wonder if they are trying to trick him

2. What will the bird most likely do if he sees food in a cage?

    (a) sing

    (b) tell his friends

    (c) leave it alone

    (d) try to eat it

3. Draw a picture to show what you think the man will do the next time he hears a bird singing at night.

Name _____

Activity: Read the story below and complete page 56.

1. Lion was walking by the sea one day when he saw Dolphin lift his head out of the water.

2. "Hello, Dolphin!" said Lion. "I am the king of the beasts. Do you want to be my friend? We could help each other."

3. "I am the king of the ocean," said Dolphin. "I would like to be your friend. I would like to be able to help you, too."

4. Soon after, Lion had a fight with a wild bull. He asked Dolphin to help him.

5. Dolphin wanted to help him, but he wasn't able to. He could not go on the land.

6. Lion was very angry. "You are not a good friend," he said. "You said you would help me!"

Name _____

Use the strategies you learned and practiced in *The Man and the Singing Bird* to help you make predictions about what may happen.

> **Remember:**
> - The answers are not in the text.
> - Find and underline information in the text to use and think about.
> - Think hard! What is the writer suggesting might happen?
> - Think about all answers before deciding.

1. What will Dolphin probably say to Lion?

    (a) "I don't want to be your friend."

    (b) "I'm coming to help."

    (c) "I'd like to help, but I can't go on the land."

    (d) "I didn't say that I wanted to be your friend."

    > **Think!**
    > Read what the animals said to each other. Then choose an answer.

2. Draw an **X** in the box by the things that Lion could do to help himself.

    (a) fight harder ☐   (b) run away ☐

    (c) bite and scratch ☐   (d) call other land animals to help ☐

3. Draw what you think will happen next.

Name _____

Activity: Read the passage below, and use pages 58–60 to show how well you can sequence, find similarities and differences, and predict.

The Chatting Elf

1.   Once upon a time in the land of Nod, there lived an elf named Jabber who liked to chat with everyone he met.

2.   First, he chatted with Mr. Cream, the milkman, who was delivering his milk when the sun was coming up. Mr. Cream was late delivering his milk.

3.   Next, he chatted with Mrs. Stout when she was hanging her laundry after breakfast. Mrs. Stout was late for her visit to the doctor.

4.   Then, he chatted with Mrs. Snoop for a long time when she poked her head over the fence at lunchtime to ask him to pick up her mail. Mrs. Snoop was late for her visit to the hairdresser.

5.   Finally, he chatted with Bill and Bob for a long time when they walked home from elf school in the afternoon. They were late getting home, and their mom was mad.

6.   They thought of a plan to stop Jabber from chatting so much. First, Mr. Cream woke Jabber up to chat very, very early in the morning. Next, Mrs. Stout chatted with him when he wanted to go shopping. The shop closed before he could do his shopping. Then, Mrs. Snoop chatted with him when he was cooking dinner, and his dinner burned. Finally, Bill and Bob chatted with Jabber when he wanted to take his dog for a walk. Barkey got angry and started barking.

7.   Jabber decided to stop chatting so much. Now, Jabber just waves to everyone as they pass his house.

Assessment

Name _____

> ### Remember:
>
> - Ask, "Which events need to be sequenced?"
> - Find the events in the text and underline them.
> - Think about how these events fit together. Look for time-marker words, like *then*, *before*, *next*, etc.
> - Check ALL the answers before deciding.

1. What did Jabber do first in the morning?

(a) He chatted with Bill and Bob.

(b) He went to bed.

(c) He cooked dinner.

(d) He chatted with Mr. Cream.

2. Who chatted with Jabber last (finally)?

(a) Mrs. Stout

(b) Bill and Bob

(c) the shopkeeper

(d) Barkey

3. Number the events in the correct story order.

(a) Mrs. Snoop made him burn dinner. ☐

(b) Bill and Bob made Barkey bark. ☐

(c) Mr. Cream woke Jabber up. ☐

(d) Mrs. Stout made him late for the shop. ☐

Name _____

> **Remember:**
> - What is the question asking for? Underline the keywords.
> - A table or chart can help you to see similarities and differences.
> - Check all answers before deciding.

1. What same thing did Jabber cause to each person he chatted with?

(a) He made them all burn their dinner.

(b) He made Barkey angry at them all.

(c) He made them all late.

(d) He made them all late for the hairdresser.

2. Draw an **X** in the boxes to show the different times of day when Jabber spoke to each person.

	Morning	Lunchtime	Afternoon
Bill and Bob			
Mrs. Stout			
Mrs. Snoop			
Mr. Cream			

3. Who did Jabber chat with at the same time of the day? Use the chart to help you.

(a) Mrs. Snoop and Mr. Cream

(b) Mrs. Stout and Mr. Cream

(c) Mrs. Stout and Mrs. Snoop

(d) Bill and Bob and Mr. Cream

Name _____

> ### Remember:
>
> - The answers are not in the text.
> - Find and underline information in the text to use and think about.
> - Think hard! What is the writer suggesting might happen?
> - Think about all answers before deciding.

1. What would have probably happened if Jabber kept chatting so much?

(a) Jabber would go to the hairdresser.

(b) Jabber would visit the doctor.

(c) Barkey wouldn't get his walks.

(d) Everyone would keep away from Jabber.

2. Write sentences to tell what probably happened when . . .

(a) Mrs. Stout was late for her visit to the doctor.

_____

_____

_____

(b) Mrs. Snoop was late getting to the hairdresser.

_____

_____

_____

Lesson Objective

- Students will make judgments and reach conclusions based on facts and/or details provided in a text.

Background Information

This section demonstrates how to decide on the meaning of facts and details provided in a text and how to build up evidence in order to make judgments and reach conclusions about the information.

Students also need to be able to search for evidence to support a particular conclusion by locating the relevant information in the text and then making judgments about it.

In higher-order comprehension skills such as this, answers are not always immediately obvious, and discussion about why one answer is judged to be the best should be encouraged. However, teachers may decide to accept another answer if a student can provide the necessary evidence to support the answer he or she has given.

Activity Answers

Boys .... **Pages 65–68**

- Practice Page: Page 67
    1. (b)
    2. (c)
    3. Answers will vary.
- On Your Own: Page 68
    1. (b)
    2. (a)
    3. These statements should be circled:
       They push in front of her.
       They take toys from her.
       They don't see her when she wants to join in.
    4. Drawings will vary.

Dogs .... **Pages 69–70**

- Try It Out: Page 70
    1. (c)
    2. (c)
    3. (b)

Assessment Answers

Drawing Conclusions .... **Page 84**

1. (c)
2. (d)
3. Answers will vary.

Lesson Objective

• Students will summarize text by linking important information and identifying the main points.

Background Information

To be able to summarize text successfully, students first need to be clear about what they are being asked to do and what form their answer should take. (For example, a one-word answer or a more detailed explanation may be required.) It will help if they underline the keywords in the question.

They then need to locate any relevant information in the text, underline it, and establish how it is linked. Words such as *while, but, and, when*, and *as* may be significant in establishing how the information is linked. Unnecessary and irrelevant information should be omitted and the main points established for inclusion in the summary.

Students may need to locate information throughout the entire text in order to summarize the main points for some questions.

Answers may vary and will require teacher review. Those given below are provided as a guide to the main points.

Activity Answers

Strange Plants .... **Pages 71–74**

• Practice Page: Page 73
  1. (a)
  2. Insects slip and <u>fall</u> down to the bottom of a deep <u>hole</u> in the <u>middle</u> of the pitcher plant and cannot <u>get</u> out.
  3. (c)
• On Your Own: Page 74
  1. (d)
  2. (a)
  3. Drawings should include a pitcher plant with an insect trapped in the middle.

Dentists .... **Pages 75–76**

• Try It Out: Page 76
  1. (d)
  2. (b)
  3. Answers will vary. Possible answer: They help you look after your teeth.

Assessment Answers

Summarizing .... **Page 85**

  1. (c)
  2. (a)
  3. (a) cut   (b) mix   (c) add
     (d) stir   (e) sprinkle   (f) refrigerate
  4. Answers will vary.

Lesson Objective

- Students will make inferences about what is most likely to be true based on information provided in the text.

Background Information

Inferences are opinions about what is most likely to be true and are formed after careful evaluation of all the available information. Students need to realize that because there is no information that tells them the actual answer, their inferences may not be correct. They have to determine what makes the most sense given the information provided and to then look for details to support their decisions. They may need to use some prior knowledge to help them to determine their answer.

The focus of this section is on teaching students how to use contextual information, both written and visual, to determine what they believe to be true. They then must find further evidence to support their decisions.

Student answers will need to be checked by the teacher, but some possible answers have been provided as a guide.

Activity Answers

My Street .... **Pages 77–80**

- Practice Page: Page 79
  1. (a)
  2. (b)
  3. (c)
- On Your Own: Page 80
  1. (d)
  2. (c)
  3. Answers should be similar to: He did not have to go to school.
  4. Drawings will vary.

Letter to Jack .... **Pages 81–82**

- Try It Out: Page 82
  1. (d)
  2. (b)
  3. Nan and Pop are the parents of Ty's mom.
  4. (c)

Assessment Answers

Making Inferences .... **Page 86**

1. (b)
2. (c)
3. Answers will vary. Possible answers could include:
   (a) make it sweeter
   (b) it is cold

Helpful Hints

DRAWING CONCLUSIONS

- Make sure you understand what it is you are drawing conclusions about.

- Look in the text to find the facts and details.

- Make decisions about what they mean.

- Always check all possible answers before deciding on your answer.

SUMMARIZING

- Check the text to be sure you understand the question. Then, find the keywords.

- Find information in the text that is most important to your understanding of it. Decide how it is connected.

- Take out any unnecessary details or unconnected information.

- Always check all possible answers before deciding on your answer.

MAKING INFERENCES

- The answers are usually not in the text, but there is information that will give you clues to think about.

- Find the answer that makes the most sense and is supported by the text.

- Always consider all possible answers before making a decision.

Name _____

When we draw conclusions, we make decisions and judgments based on details provided in the text.

Activity: Read the letter below and complete pages 66–68.

Dear Clara,

1. My brothers have not been treating me well lately. Let me tell you what is going on.

2. They play noisy games with cars, trucks, and trains. They make a lot of noise when they play outside. They even make a lot of noise when they do schoolwork and play board games. Boys are noisy!

3. Boys are mean. When we stand in line at the store, my brothers try to push in front of me. Sometimes they don't even see me when I ask if I can join their game. Other times they take toys from me when I am playing with them.

4. My brothers forget to put away their things. They leave trash behind after they eat. They don't hang up their clothes or towels. They don't put away their toys. They like to play in mud and sand and make a mess. Boys are messy.

5. They like football, silly cartoons, bugs, fighting, and books about aliens. Boys don't like good things!

6. I have decided that boys are not nice people!

Your friend,
Lucy

Name _____

Follow the steps below to learn how to draw conclusions.

> - Conclusions are decisions you make about the meaning of details in the text.
> - Find out what you are making conclusions about.
> - Look in the text to find the details. Underline them.
> - Make decisions about what they mean.
> - Check all answers before deciding.

Step 1: Read the question.

Why does the girl think that boys are mean?

(a) because her brothers forget to put away their clothes

(b) because her brothers play in mud and sand

(c) because her brothers like fighting

(d) because her brothers push in front of her and take her toys

Step 2: You will need to find the word ***mean*** in paragraph 3. Underline the things she says her brothers do that are mean.

Step 3: Choose the best answer by thinking about each choice carefully.

(a) She says her brothers don't hang up their clothes. This is not why she thinks they are mean. This is not a good answer.

(b) She says they play in mud and sand. This is not why she thinks they are mean. This is not a good answer.

(c) She says they fight. Fighting is a mean thing to do. Is this the best answer? You must check all answers.

(d) In paragraph 3, she says boys are mean because her brothers push in front of her and take her toys. This is the best answer.

Drawing Conclusions

Name _____

Practice drawing conclusions. Use the clues in the "Think!" boxes to help you.

1. Why does the girl think that boys are not nice people?

(a) because some boys in her class pushed her

(b) because her brothers are not being nice to her

(c) because her brothers took her lunch without asking

(d) because she doesn't like the things boys like

> **Think!**
> Who is bothering her and why?

2. The girl says that boys don't like good things. She says this is because:

(a) they like quiet games.

(b) they like trucks and trains.

(c) they like silly cartoons and bugs.

(d) they like being neat.

> **Think!**
> Read paragraph 5. Underline the things boys like.

3. How do you think the girl would feel about boys if her brothers treated her better?

> **Think!**
> What if her brothers were very nice to her?

_____

_____

_____

_____

Name _____

Use the strategies you have been practing to help you draw conclusions.

1. Does the girl writing the letter like boys?

   (a) yes   (b) no   (c) don't know   (d) sometimes

2. Because the boys leave trash behind and don't put away their toys, the girl thinks they are:

   (a) messy.   (b) mean.   (c) noisy.   (d) silly.

3. Circle the boxes that say why the girl thinks boys are mean.

They push in front of her.	They like books about aliens.	They take toys from her.
They play in the mud.	They don't see her when she wants to join in.	They play noisy games.

4. Draw a picture to show why the girl thinks boys are noisy.

Name _____

Activity: Read the poem below and complete page 70.

DOGS

1.   Dogs are animals that make good pets.

   You need to find out what kind to get!

   Some are big, and some are small.

   Just choose the breed you like—that's all!

2.   Dogs do need a lot of care.

   A bed, a leash, a brush for their hair,

   Some food and water and a walk,

   A ball or toy and someone to talk.

3.   Dogs wag their tails and lick your face.

   They follow you all over the place.

   Dogs give people so much love.

   That is something I'm very sure of!

4.   A dog would make a really great pet.

   Have you decided to get one yet?

Name _____

Use the strategies you learned and practiced in *Boys* to help you with drawing conclusions.

Remember:
- Conclusions are decisions that you make about the meaning of facts and details in the text.
- Find what you are making conclusions about.
- Look in the text to find the facts and details. Underline them.
- Make decisions about what they mean.
- Check all answers before deciding.

1. Why does the writer conclude that dogs love people?

(a) They will go for walks.

(b) They like food.

(c) They wag their tails and follow you.

(d) They are good pets.

Think!
Find the word *love* in stanza 3.

2. The best conclusion for stanza 2 would be:

(a) Dogs bark a lot.

(b) Dogs don't take up very much space.

(c) Dogs need a lot of care.

(d) Dogs have fleas.

3. Which conclusion would be best for stanza 1?

(a) Dogs are clever.

(b) There are lots of different dogs to choose from.

(c) Dogs are big.

(d) Dogs don't need a lot of care.

Name _____

Summarizing is stating the main ideas or facts without using many words. Summarizing can help us to understand text.

Activity: Read the passage below and complete pages 72–74.

Strange Plants

1.   A pitcher plant is a meat-eating plant—a carnivore! These plants eat lots of insects that get trapped in them.

2.   Pitcher plants can have lovely colors. They can have nice smells. They can have sticky nectar. These attract insects to them.

3.   Pitcher plants have a deep hole in the middle like a cup. When insects are trapped inside the plants, they slip on the walls and fall down to the bottom. They cannot get out.

4.   Pitcher plants have a pool of special water at the bottom. When the insects fall into the water, they drown. The water "eats" the insects. It takes two or three days to do this.

5.   Pitcher plants grow in poor soil where other plants cannot grow. They cannot get food from the soil, so they catch their own food to eat.

6.   Pitcher plants can grow by climbing up trees. They can grow on the ground in forests. They can grow by attaching themselves to trees.

7.   Pitcher plants are clever but strange plants.

Name _____

Follow the steps below to learn how to identify the main points and summarize text.

> • Make sure you understand the question. Underline the keywords.
> • Look for information in the text. Decide what is important and how it is connected.
> • Leave out any information you don't need.
> • Check all the answers before deciding.

Step 1: Read the question.

Which sentence best summarizes paragraph 1?

(a) Pitcher plants eat meat.

(b) Pitcher plants trap insects.

(c) Pitcher plants eat insects.

(d) Pitcher plants are meat-eating plants that trap insects.

Step 2: The keywords in the question are ***best summarizes***. Underline that part of the question. Read the first paragraph and underline the keywords in each sentence. Decide which information would not be needed in the summary.

Step 3: Choose the best answer by thinking about each choice carefully. Look for the sentence that gives all the important information.

(a) It does say this in paragraph 1, but important information has been left out. This is not a good answer.

(b) It does say this in paragraph 1, but important information has been left out. This is not a good answer.

(c) It does say this in paragraph 1, but important information has been left out. This is not a good answer.

(d) This sentence gives all the important information. It is the best answer.

Name _____

Practice summarizing. Use the clues in the "Think!" boxes to help you.

1. Which sentence best summarizes the information in paragraph 2?

    (a) Pitcher plants use different ways to attract insects.

    (b) Pitcher plants are pretty.

    (c) Pitcher plants have to catch their own food.

    (d) Pitcher plants get food from the soil.

> **Think!**
> Read paragraph 2 carefully and decide what it is telling you about.

2. Complete the summary of paragraph 3.

    Insects slip and _____ down to the

    bottom of a deep _____ in the

    _____ of the pitcher plant and cannot

    _____ out.

> **Think!**
> Read paragraph 3 carefully and think about the words.

3. Draw an **X** in the box that gives the best summary about paragraph 4.

    (a) Pitcher plants collect water. ☐

    (b) Pitcher plants like to eat spiders. ☐

    (c) Special water in pitcher plants "eats" insects. ☐

    (d) Insects like pitcher plants. ☐

> **Think!**
> Read paragraph 4 carefully. Find some keywords. Underline them.

Name _____

Use the strategies you have been practicing to help you summarize text.

1. Which sentence summarizes paragraph 5 best?

    (a) Pitcher plants are very hungry plants.

    (b) Pitcher plants have spines.

    (c) Pitcher plants have a cup in the middle.

    (d) Pitcher plants need to catch their own food.

2. Choose the best answer. Paragraph 6 gives information about:

    (a) where and how pitcher plants grow.

    (b) what pitcher plants look like.

    (c) how pitcher plants make seeds.

    (d) the parts of a pitcher plant.

3. Draw a diagram that summarizes how pitcher plants eat.

Name _____

Activity: Read the passage below and complete page 76.

DENTISTS

1.   Dentists have a very important job. They help you look after your teeth.

2.   Dentists have to look at your teeth, mouth, and gums. If something is wrong, they plan out what to do about it.

3.   Dentists fill holes in teeth. They can make teeth straight. They take x-rays of teeth. They fix broken teeth. Dentists take out teeth. They order false teeth. They put fluoride on teeth to make them strong.

4.   Dentists tell people what food to eat for strong, healthy teeth. They show people how to brush and floss and look after their teeth.

5.   Dentists sometimes give their patients special shots or gas to keep them comfortable while they work on their teeth. They can also give medicine to help people with infections or pain.

6.   Dentists use lots of things such as x-ray machines, drills, mouth mirrors, probes, brushes, and needles. They must wear gloves and masks to protect themselves and their patients from infections.

Name _____

Use the strategies you learned and practiced in *Strange Plants* to help you summarize information.

> **Remember:**
> - Make sure you understand the question. Underline the keywords.
> - Look for information in the text. Decide what is important and how it is connected.
> - Leave out any information you don't need.
> - Check all the answers before deciding.

1. Which is the best summary of paragraph 4?

(a) Dentists make a lot of money.

(b) Dentists are friendly people.

(c) Dentists use lots of equipment.

(d) Dentists tell you how to keep your teeth healthy.

> **Think!**
> Read paragraph 4 carefully. There are words in the text to help you.

2. Paragraph 6 mainly tells about:

(a) different things that can go wrong with teeth.

(b) different things that dentists use.

(c) different ways dentists fix teeth.

(d) how to look after your teeth.

3. Why do you think dentists have an important job?

_____

_____

Making Inferences

Name _____

When we read, we often decide what we think might be true based on information in the text. This is called *making inferences*.

Activity: Read the story below and complete pages 78–80.

My Street

1. On Monday morning, I walked down my street with Mom to school. I met my friends at school. We learned lots of things and played games.

2. On Monday afternoon, I walked back up the street to go home.

3. On Tuesday morning, I walked down my street to school.

4. On Tuesday afternoon, I drove up my street to go to piano lessons.

5. On Wednesday morning, I ran down my street to school. We had to hurry.

6. On Wednesday afternoon, I walked up my street to go to Brock's house to play.

7. On Thursday morning, I walked down my street to school. We learned lots of things and sang songs.

8. On Thursday night, we drove up my street to go shopping. We ate take-out in the food court.

9. On Friday morning, we walked slowly to school. We looked at the new house being built and the nice gardens.

10. On Friday night, I stayed up late and watched a movie.

11. I didn't walk down my street on Saturday and Sunday.

Name _____

Follow the steps below to learn how to make inferences.

- The answers are usually not in the text, but there is information to give you clues to think about. (This could be underlined.)
- Find the answer that makes the most sense and is supported by details from the text.
- Consider all answers before deciding.

Step 1: Read the question.

Why did the child walk to school with his mom?

(a) He liked walking and talking with his friends.

(b) He wanted to stretch his new shoes.

(c) His mom wanted to get some exercise.

(d) His mom wanted him to get to school safely.

Step 2: The question asks about walking to school with an adult. Think about why adults would want to walk to school with their children.

Step 3: Choose the best answer by thinking about each choice carefully. Look for the answer that makes the most sense.

(a) The child met his friends at school. They did not walk with him and his mom to school. This is not the best answer.

(b) This answer talks about new shoes. New shoes are not talked about at all in the text. This is not a good answer.

(c) Lots of moms like to exercise so this may be true. This may be a good answer, but remember to read all of them as there may be a better answer.

(d) Keeping children safe is very important to moms and dads. This child is probably not old enough to walk to school by himself. This is probably the best answer.

Making Inferences

Name _____

Practice making inferences. Use the clues in the "Think!" boxes to help you.

1. What would be the best reason why they drove to piano lessons?

   (a) It was too far to walk.

   (b) The car engine needed to be used.

   (c) They had to carry the piano in the car.

   (d) They liked using the car to go everywhere.

   Think!
   Read and think about all the answers.

2. Where was the food court where they ate on Thursday night?

   (a) a long way from the shops

   (b) at the shopping center

   (c) at their house

   (d) next to the school

   Think!
   Find the words **food court** and read about what they did on Thursday night.

3. What would be the best reason why they ran to school on Wednesday morning?

   (a) They wanted to get fit.

   (b) They liked running.

   (c) They were late.

   (d) They had new running shoes to try.

   Think!
   Read paragraph 5. Then think why people have to hurry to places.

Name _____

Use the strategies you have been practicing to help you make inferences.

1. Why did they probably have the time on Friday morning to walk slowly and look at things?

    (a) They were late for school.

    (b) They had to get up early to go to piano lessons.

    (c) They had to go to Brock's house.

    (d) They started walking to school early.

2. What would be the best reason why the child was able to stay up late on Friday night?

    (a) There was a good movie on television.

    (b) His friends came to his house.

    (c) He did not have to get up to go to school the next day.

    (d) He did not sleep well on Friday nights.

3. Write a sentence to tell the best reason why the child did not walk down his street on Saturday and Sunday.

    _____

    _____

4. Think about what the child does at school. Draw a picture to show how you think he feels about school.

Name _____

Activity: Read the letter below and complete page 82.

Letter to Jack

Dear Jack,

1.   It was 9 o'clock in the morning when Nan and Pop picked me up from the airport. They hugged and kissed me.

2.   We climbed into the old truck and drove out of town. The road was covered with red dust. Stumpy bushes grew along the side of the road. I saw brown rabbits hopping along and cattle standing around. The sky was as blue as the sea. There wasn't one cloud in the sky.

3.   Finally, we turned onto a gravel road and drove through a set of wide gates. Two big posts stood on either side. The large sign across the posts said "Rabbit Flats Station."

4.   We parked the truck in the shed next to the tractor and went into the house. Pop put my suitcase in Mom's old bedroom. In the kitchen, Nan poured tall glasses of lemonade and put out a big plate of scones with jam and cream.

5.   Yobbo sniffed around my feet looking for scraps while I ate my snack.

6.   While Nan washed the dishes and put away the leftovers, I gazed out the window at the horses.

7.   This vacation is going to be so much fun! Wish you were here, Jack. I guess I'll have to eat all of Nan's great cooking by myself.

Love,
Ty

Name _____

Use the strategies you learned and practiced in *My Street* to help you practice inferring.

Remember:

- The answers are usually not in the text, but there is information to give you clues to think about. (This could be underlined.)
- Find the answer that makes the most sense and is supported by details from the text.
- Consider all answers before deciding.

1. Where do Ty's Nan and Pop most likely live?

(a) near the beach

(b) in a snowy area

(c) in the city

(d) in a dry area

Think!
Read paragraph 2.

2. Rabbit Flats Station is:

(a) a train station.

(b) a cattle station.

(c) a gas station.

(d) a fire station.

3. Whose mom and dad are Nan and Pop?

_____

4. Most likely, who is Jack?

(a) Ty's teacher

(b) Ty's mom

(c) Ty's brother

(d) Ty's pet rabbit

Name _____

Activity: Read the recipe below and use pages 84–86 to show how well you can draw conclusions, summarize, and make inferences.

Make Fabulous Fruit Salad

You will need:

- 1 green apple
- 1 mango
- 3 slices of cantaloupe
- 1 basket of strawberries
- large bowl
- spoon
- small can of pineapple pieces with juice

- 1 red apple
- 1 peach
- mint sprigs
- sugar
- knife
- cutting board

Steps:

(1) Cut all the fruit into small pieces except for the pineapple.

(2) Mix them together carefully in a large bowl.

(3) Add mint sprigs and the pineapple pieces with juice.

(4) Stir together gently.

(5) Sprinkle lightly with sugar.

(6) Refrigerate until cool.

Test:

Enjoy on a hot summer day.

Name _____

Remember:

- Decide what it is you are making conclusions about.
- Look in the text to find the facts and details. Underline them.
- Make decisions about what they mean.
- Check all the answers before deciding.

---

1. Why does the fruit need to be cut up?

(a) to make it taste better

(b) to make it easy to cook

(c) to make it easy to eat

(d) to peel it

2. Sugar is added:

(a) to look good.

(b) to make it cold.

(c) to add color.

(d) to make it sweeter.

3. Read each statement. Write **yes** or **no**.

(a) The ingredients are hard to find.   _____

(b) This recipe is hard to make.   _____

(c) This would make a lot of fruit salad.   _____

(d) This fruit salad would be colorful.   _____

(e) I would like this fruit salad.   _____

Summarizing

Name _____

> ## Remember:
>
> - Make sure you understand the question. Underline the keywords.
> - Look for information in the text. Decide what is important and how it is connected.
> - Leave out any information you don't need.
> - Check all the answers before deciding.

1. Which word best summarizes everything that goes into the fruit salad?

   (a) cereal   (b) spices

   (c) fruit   (d) meat

2. Which word best summarizes all the other things needed to make the fruit salad?

   (a) utensils   (b) food

   (c) animals   (d) books

3. Copy words from the text to summarize the steps taken to make fruit salad. The start of each word is given.

   (a) c_____   (b) m_____   (c) a_____

   (d) st_____   (e) sp_____   (f) r_____

4. Complete the sentence.

   I think fruit salad is _____.

Name _____

> **Remember:**
>
> - The answers are usually not in the text, but there is information to give you clues to think about. (This could be underlined.)
> - Find the answer that makes the most sense and is supported by details from the text.
> - Check all the answers before deciding.

1. Where could the fruit be placed while it is being cut up?

    (a) bowl   (b) cutting board

    (c) spoon   (d) mat

2. What is the fruit mixed and stirred with?

    (a) knife   (b) cutting board

    (c) spoon   (d) fork

3. Complete the sentences.

    (a) The fruit salad can be sprinkled with sugar to . . .

_____

_____.

    (b) The fruit salad would be good to enjoy on a hot summer day

    because _____

_____.

Lesson Objective

• Students will determine cause and effect and understand how they are connected.

Background Information

Students need to understand that a cause leads to an effect and that they are connected.

This section demonstrates strategies for students to use in order to find information in a text, which in turn helps them to make the connection and determine cause and effect.

They need to find and underline the keywords in questions, and then search for information in the text that makes connections between the keywords and either the cause or the effect. They need to understand that they will be given either a cause or an effect in the question, but they will need to search for the other.

Activity Answers

One to Five .... **Pages 91–94**

• Practice Page: Page 93
  1. (a)
  2. (b)
  3. (a) effect   (b) cause   (c) effect   (d) cause   (e) effect   (f) cause
• On Your Own: Page 94
  1. (c)
  2. (c)
  3. (a) ... her new shoe was slippery.
     (b) ... he tripped on the tree.

The Sandman .... **Pages 95–96**

• Try It Out: Page 96
  1. (a)
  2. (b)
  3. (a) holds an umbrella with pictures on it over them
     (b) holds an umbrella over them that has no pictures on it

Assessment Answers

Cause and Effect .... **Page 110**

  1. (a)
  2. (b)
  3. (a) I cried   (b) barked   (c) he dragged it all over the yard

Lesson Objective

- Students will demonstrate their ability to identify facts and opinions and their understanding of how they differ.

Background Information

A fact is something that is true. It can be verified by referring to other information. In other words, it can be checked and be proven to be correct.

An opinion is something that someone believes to be true but cannot be verified. In other words, it is something that someone *thinks* rather than knows is true.

Students must be able to distinguish between facts and opinions in order to become critical readers. They have to engage and interact with text and read with a questioning attitude. They can then look for relationships and critically judge and evaluate what they read by identifying facts and opinions.

Critical readers become more discriminating consumers of the news media and advertising—an important life skill.

Activity Answers

Homes .... **Pages 97–100**
- Practice Page: Page 99
  1. (a)
  2. (b)
  3. (a) fact   (b) opinion
- On Your Own: Page 100
  1. (c)
  2. (d)
  3. (a) fact   (b) opinion   (c) fact

Showbags .... **Pages 101–102**
- Try It Out: Page 102
  1. (a)
  2. (d)
  3. opinion

Assessment Answers

Fact or Opinion .... **Page 111**
  1. (c)
  2. (b)
  3. (a) fact   (b) fact

Lesson Objective

- Students will understand and identify the writer's point of view and purpose.

Background Information

The writer's point of view is his or her opinion about a subject. A reader should, after careful and detailed analysis of what has been written, understand and be able to identify the point of view expressed in the text.

The writer's purpose for writing explains why the text was written. It may be to express a particular point of view, to amuse, entertain, inform, persuade, instruct, describe, record information, or to explain something.

Students should be encouraged to try to determine how and what the writer was thinking and use this to help them make decisions about the writer's point of view. They should then look for details in the text to support or reject the choices they have made. (These can be underlined.)

All possible choices should be considered before a final decision is made.

Activity Answers

How Jellyfish Look After Themselves .... Pages 103–106

- Practice Page: Page 105
    1. (a)
    2. (b)
    3. it puts poison into its prey
- On Your Own: Page 106
    1. (b)
    2. (a)
    3. (c)
    4. Answers will vary.

Jack and the Beanstalk .... Pages 107–108

- Try It Out: Page 108
    1. (a)
    2. (a) silly   (b) brave   (c) liked
    3. (d)

Assessment Answers

Point of View and Purpose .... Page 112
    1. (b)
    2. (d)
    3. (b)

Helpful Hints

CAUSE AND EFFECT

- A cause (what happened first) leads to an effect (what happened as a result of the cause). They are connected.

- You are given either a cause or an effect, and you will need to find the other.

- Look for keywords in the question. Then, find the words in the text that are connected to the keywords.

- Check all possible answers before making a decision.

FACT OR OPINION

- A fact is something that can be checked and proven to be correct.

- An opinion is what someone believes to be true, but it can't be proven. Read the text to decide what can be proven (fact) by the text.

- Always check all possible answers before deciding on your answer.

POINT OF VIEW AND PURPOSE

- Writers do not always tell you what they believe. You may have to come to this conclusion based on the information you have read.

- Look for details and information in the text to help you decide why the author may have written the text or what the author's point of view is.

- Always check all possible answers before deciding on your answer.

Name _____

Cause and effect is a phrase we use to explain when one thing (a cause) makes something else happen (an effect). Identifying cause and effect will help you understand what you read.

Activity: Read the poem below and complete pages 92–94.

One to Five

1.   When Jamal was one
       He learned how to run.
    When the dog took his bun
       He didn't run for fun.

2.   When Maria was two
       She tripped on her shoe.
          It was brand new.
       It was slippery and blue.

3.   When Jai was three
       He fell on his knee.
    He tripped on the tree
       Which he did not see.

4.   When Su-Li was four
       Her head hit the door.
    She fell down on the floor
       And felt very sore.

5.   When Mario was five
       He learned how to dive.
          Bees from a hive
       Tried to eat him alive.

Name _____

Follow the steps below to learn how to identify cause and effect.

> • A cause leads to an effect. They are joined together.
> • You will be told one, and you will need to identify the other.
> • Look for keywords in the question and underline them.
> • Find words in the text that are joined to the keywords in the question.
> • Check all answers before deciding.

Step 1: Read the question.

What caused Jamal to run?

(a) He was chasing bees.

(b) He was in a race.

(c) His mom was chasing him.

(d) He chased the dog that took his bun.

Step 2: The keywords in the question are *Jamal* and *run*. Underline them in the question. Find the keywords in the same stanza in the poem. Underline them.

Step 3: Choose the best answer by thinking about each choice carefully.

(a) The bees are talked about later in the poem, but it was Mario who was chased by the bees. This is not the best answer.

(b) The poem does not say anything about Jamal being in a race. This is not a good answer.

(c) The poem does not say anything about Jamal's mom at all. This is not a good answer.

(d) The first stanza tells about Jamal learning to run when the dog took his bun. He did not run for fun. This is the best answer.

Cause and Effect

Name _____

Practice finding cause and effect. Use the clues in the "Think!" boxes to help you.

1. What caused Maria to trip over her shoe?

    (a) The shoes were slippery and new.

    (b) She ran after the dog.

    (c) She did not tie her shoelace.

    (d) The shoe was too big for her.

> **Think!**
> Find and read the stanza where Maria and her shoe are talked about. The cause is in the same stanza.

2. What caused Jai to fall on his knee?

    (a) He twisted his ankle.

    (b) He tripped on the tree.

    (c) He slipped on the floor.

    (d) He tripped over Jamal's foot.

> **Think!**
> Find and read the stanza that tells about Jai. Find the cause.

3. Read each statement. Write **cause** or **effect** for each.

> **Think!**
> Think about what caused something to happen.

    (a) Jamal learned how to run.   _____

    (b) The dog took his bun.   _____

    (c) Maria tripped on her shoe.   _____

    (d) Her new shoe was slippery.   _____

    (e) Jai fell on his knee.   _____

    (f) He tripped on the tree.   _____

Name _____

Use the strategies you have been practicing to help you identify cause and effect.

1. What caused Su-Li to feel very sore?

   (a) She cut her finger.

   (b) She bumped her foot.

   (c) She fell down on the floor and hit her head on the door.

   (d) She tripped on her new, blue shoe.

2. What caused Mario to learn to dive?

   (a) He was swimming with his dad.

   (b) He was in a submarine.

   (c) Bees from a hive tried to eat him alive.

   (d) He tripped on a tree.

3. Copy words from the poem to write the cause to match each effect.

   (a) Maria tripped on her shoe because. . .

   _____

   _____.

   (b) Jai fell on his knee because . . .

   _____

   _____.

Name _____

Activity: Read the story below and complete page 96.

The Sandman

1. The Sandman visits children at nighttime.

2. He takes off his shoes and walks in his socks so he doesn't make any noise.

3. He opens doors without making any noise.

4. The Sandman sneaks behind children and blows special dust onto their necks to make them sleepy.

5. He also throws the special dust into children's eyes so that they can't open them and see him.

6. He likes children. He only wants them to be quiet while he tells them stories.

7. He holds up an umbrella with pictures on it over good children. They dream beautiful stories all night.

8. He holds up an umbrella with no pictures on it over bad children. They sleep all night without having any dreams.

9. In the morning, the children wake up. They have to wipe sleep dust from their eyes because the Sandman has paid them a visit during the night.

Name _____

Use the strategies you learned and practiced in *One to Five* to help you identify cause and effect.

Remember:
- A cause leads to an effect. They are joined together.
- You will be told one, and you will need to identify the other.
- Look for keywords in the question. Underline them.
- Find words in the text that are joined to the keywords in the question.
- Check all answers before deciding.

Think!
Read paragraph 2.

1. What is the effect of the Sandman taking off his shoes and walking in his socks?

(a) He makes no noise.　(b) He does not slip on the floor.

(c) He hides the holes.　(d) His feet do not smell so much.

2. Why can't the children open their eyes?

(a) He glues them shut.　(b) He throws special dust in their eyes.

(c) He tapes them shut.　(d) They are too scared to open them.

3. Complete the sentences.

(a) Good children dream beautiful dreams because he . . .

_____

_____.

(b) Bad children have no dreams because he . . .

_____

_____.

Fact or Opinion

Name _____

A fact is something that is true. An opinion is something that someone *thinks* is true. When reading, it is important to understand the difference between facts and opinions and to determine which is which.

Activity: Read the passage below and complete pages 98–100.

HOMES

1. A home is a building where people live.

2. Homes have a roof and walls. Roofs can be made of grass, wood, metal, tiles, or other things. A tile roof looks the best.

3. Homes can be made of brick, grass, ice, timber, or other material. Brick is the best material for building homes.

4. Homes have rooms to do different things in. Some homes have many rooms. Some have only a few rooms. A home with lots of rooms would be good for a big family.

5. Homes can be big or small. Small homes are easier to look after than big homes.

6. Some homes have a yard. My big backyard is good.

7. Homes like castles or igloos stay in one place. Homes like caravans, boats, or tents can be moved around. A home that moves would be fun to live in.

8. Homes can have a garage or a carport for cars. A home with a garage is better because you can lock it up.

9. People need homes to keep them safe from rain, wind, heat, and cold.

10. I'm glad I've got my home to live in!

Name _____

Follow the steps below to learn how to determine if something is a fact or an opinion.

> • Ask yourself:
>   Can the statement be checked and proven to be correct? If it can, it's a fact.
>   Is it what someone *thinks* is true and can't be proven? If so, it's an opinion.
>   For example: Hens lay eggs. (fact)
>   Eggs taste good. (opinion)
> • Check all the answers before deciding.

Step 1: Read the question.

Which sentence is an opinion?

(a) Homes have a roof and walls.

(b) Roofs can be made of grass, wood, metal, tiles, or other things.

(c) Homes need roofs.

(d) A tile roof looks the best.

Step 2: Choose the best answer by thinking about each choice carefully.

(a) This is a fact that would be easy to check. This is not a good answer.

(b) This information could be checked in books or on the Internet. These are facts. This is not a good answer for the question.

(c) This information could be proven and is a fact. This is not a good answer.

(d) This sentence does not give information that can be proven. This is an opinion. This is the best answer.

Fact or Opinion

Name _____

Practice identifying facts and opinions. Use the clues in the "Think!" boxes to help you.

1. Which sentence is a fact?

   (a) Homes can be made of brick, grass, ice, timber, or other material.

   (b) Homes look nice with a garden.

   (c) All homes should be made of grass.

   (d) All homes should be made of timber.

> **Think!**
> Which ones tell what someone *thinks* and cannot be proven?

2. Which sentence is an opinion?

   (a) Bricks are made of clay.

   (b) Brick is the best material for building homes.

   (c) Homes can be made of brick.

   (d) Bricks can be used to build walls.

> **Think!**
> Find the ones that are facts first and can be proven. The one left should be an opinion!

3. Write **fact** or **opinion** for each sentence.

   (a) Homes have rooms to do different things in.

   _____

   (b) A home with lots of rooms would be good for a big family.

   _____

> **Think!**
> Read each sentence carefully and think about it.

Name _____

Use the strategies you have been practicing to help you determine fact or opinion.

1. Which sentence is a fact?

   (a) Small homes are easier to look after than big homes.

   (b) Small homes are cute.

   (c) Homes can be big or small.

   (d) My big backyard is good.

2. Which sentence is an opinion?

   (a) Homes like castles or igloos stay in one place.

   (b) Homes like caravans, boats, or tents can be moved around.

   (c) A home is a building where people live.

   (d) A home that moves would be fun to live in.

3. Write *fact* or *opinion* below each sentence.

   (a) Homes can have a garage or a carport for cars.

   _____

   (b) A home with a garage is better because you can lock it up.

   _____

   (c) Homes keep people safe from rain, wind, heat, and cold.

   _____

Name _____

Activity: Read the story below and complete page 102.

Showbags

1.   Did you know that in Australia, fairs and carnivals are called "shows"? I learned this when I went there on vacation. My family had a lot of fun at this fair.

2.   Showbags are big, colorful bags full of goodies that are sold at the fair. Showbags are the best things to buy at the fair. Everyone who goes should buy a showbag.

3.   There are lots of different kinds of showbags. Some are big. They have lots of things in them. Some are small. They only have a few things in them. I like the big ones best because you get lots of goodies. Everyone should buy big showbags.

4.   Some showbags can cost a lot. Some don't cost very much at all. It is better to save up your money and buy one that costs a lot because you get lots of things in it.

5.   Showbags can be filled with comic books, little plastic toys, sweets, drinks, games, stickers, masks, balloons, and other goodies. The ones filled with chocolate and sweets are the best. Everyone should buy the showbags filled with lots of sweets and chocolates.

6.   Showbags are not too heavy to carry around. You need to buy the best ones first before they sell out. If you have enough money you can buy a few showbags to take home.

7.   Everyone should buy showbags when they go to the fair in Australia.

Name _____

Use the strategies you learned and practiced in *Homes* to help you distinguish between facts and opinions.

Remember:
- A fact can be checked and proven to be correct.
- An opinion is what someone *thinks* is true. It can't be proven.
- Check all the answers before deciding.

---

1. Which sentence is a fact?

   (a) Showbags are big, colorful bags full of goodies that are sold at the fair.

   (b) Showbags are the best things to buy at the fair.

   (c) Everyone should buy big showbags.

   (d) Everyone who goes should buy a showbag.

> **Think!**
> Which one can be proven to be true?

2. Which sentence is an opinion?

   (a) Some showbags are small.

   (b) Some showbags are big.

   (c) Some showbags can cost a lot.

   (d) It is best to buy a showbag that costs a lot.

3. Write *fact* or *opinion* for the sentence.

The ones filled with chocolate and sweets are the best.

_____

Name _____

When we read, we should try to think like the writer. Then, we can try to determine how and what he or she feels and believes (the writer's point of view). We should also think about why he or she wrote the text (the writer's purpose).

Activity: Read the passage below and complete pages 104–106.

How Jellyfish Look After Themselves

1.   Jellyfish are very unusual animals. They don't have eyes, a brain, bones, or a heart. They can sense light and smell things to figure out where they are.

2.   Jellyfish have clever ways of protecting themselves. They have bodies you can see through. This makes it easy for them to hide from animals wanting to catch and eat them. Some turtles, fish, sea snails, and slugs eat jellyfish. Healthy jellyfish can grow new parts of their tentacles if they are injured.

3.   Jellyfish sting with their tentacles. They sting animals to catch and eat them. When a jellyfish stings, it puts poison into its prey. They also use their tentacles to fight other animals. Jellyfish can be dangerous for other animals to meet in the sea.

4.   Jellyfish eat waterplants and tiny sea creatures. Bigger jellyfish can sometimes eat small fish and prawns. Jellyfish can be nasty because they even eat smaller jellyfish!

5.   Jellyfish do not often mean to hurt humans, and they tend to move away from swimmers. People who are hurt by jellyfish are usually stung by accident because they have disturbed a jellyfish.

Name _____

Follow the steps below to learn how to identify the writer's point of view and his or her probable purpose or reason for writing the text.

- Writers don't always just tell you what they think or believe or why they have written the text. Sometimes you have to try to think like they do and come to this conclusion based on the information you've read.
- In the text, there are details and information for you to find, underline, and use in making your choices.
- Check all answers before deciding.

Step 1: Read the question.

What does the writer think that jellyfish are often dangerous to?

(a) people

(b) swimmers

(c) birds

(d) small sea animals

Step 2: Choose the best answer by thinking about each choice carefully.

(a) In paragraph 5, the writer says that jellyfish do not often hurt humans. This is probably not the best answer.

(b) A swimmer could disturb a jellyfish, but it would try to move away. This is probably not the best answer.

(c) The writer doesn't say anything about birds. This is not a good answer.

(d) The writer says that jellyfish eat tiny sea animals so jellyfish would be dangerous for them. This is the best answer.

Name _____

Practice identifying the writer's point of view and why he or she wrote the text. Use the clues in the "Think!" boxes to help you.

1. The writer believes that:

   (a) jellyfish can be dangerous animals.

   (b) jellyfish are friendly animals to play with in the sea.

   (c) jellyfish make good pets.

   (d) jellyfish can be kept in a fish tank.

> **Think!**
> Read the information in paragraph 3.

2. The writer believes that:

   (a) jellyfish are funny.

   (b) jellyfish have a clever way of protecting themselves.

   (c) jellyfish have no way of protecting themselves.

   (d) jellyfish can do tricks.

> **Think!**
> Read the information in paragraph 2.

3. Complete the sentence.

The writer thinks that jellyfish are dangerous because when a jellyfish stings an animal, . . .

> **Think!**
> Find and read a paragraph that tells about this.

_____

_____.

On Your Own

Name _____

Use the strategies you have been practicing to help you identify the writer's point of view and purpose for writing the text.

1. The writer thinks jellyfish are clever, because:

    (a) they are good swimmers.

    (b) they can grow new parts.

    (c) they eat each other.

    (d) they sting people.

2. What does the writer think about jellyfish?

    (a) They are interesting and unusual.

    (b) They shouldn't sting.

    (c) They should be caught.

    (d) They make good pets.

3. Most likely, the writer wrote the text:

    (a) so people will be careful of jellyfish.

    (b) to make people frightened of jellyfish.

    (c) because jellyfish are interesting and unusual.

    (d) because he or she doesn't like jellyfish.

4. Write a sentence to tell your own point of view about jellyfish.

    _____

Text 2

Name _____

Activity: Read the passage below and complete page 108.

Jack and the Beanstalk

1. "Jack and the Beanstalk" is a well-known fairy tale.

2. It was sad that Jack and his mother were poor and had no food to eat.

3. But Jack was silly to swap the cow for magic beans.

4. I can understand why his mother got angry and threw the magic beans out the window.

5. Jack was very brave to climb up the tall beanstalk into the sky.

6. I liked the giant's rhyme when he said,

    "Fee! Fie! Foe! Fum!

    I smell the blood of an Englishman.

    Be he alive, or be he dead,

    I'll grind his bones to make my bread."

7. The giant's wife was very brave to help Jack, but he was very bad to steal the hen and the singing harp from the giant.

8. I didn't like Jack when he chopped down the beanstalk with his ax and ended the giant's life. The giant was only looking after his things.

Name _____

Use the strategies you learned and practiced in *How Jellyfish Look After Themselves* to help you identify the writer's point of view and purpose.

Remember

- Writers don't always tell you what they think or why they have written the text. You have to try to think like they do and come to this conclusion based on the information you've read.
- In the text, there are details and information about the question to find, underline, and use to make your choices.
- Check all answers before deciding.

---

1. What does the writer think about Jack and his mother being poor?

   (a) It was sad.   (b) It was a good thing.

   (c) It was funny.   (d) It was nice.

   Think!
   Read paragraph 2.

2. Complete the sentences to show what the writer thinks.

   (a) Jack was _____ to swap the cow for beans.

   (b) Jack was _____ to climb up the beanstalk.

   (c) The writer _____ the giant's rhyme.

3. Most likely, what is the best reason why the writer wrote the passage?

   (a) to tell the story

   (b) because he or she was happy

   (c) because he or she was sad

   (d) to tell what he or she thinks about the story

Name _____

Activity: Read the story below, and use pages 110–112 to show how well you can recognize cause and effect, fact or opinion, and point of view and purpose.

My Dog, Barkly

1. Yesterday, my dog, Barkly, died at the vet's office. He was a very old dog.

2. I was very sad so I cried. My brother, Max, cried, too. We loved Barkly very much. He was a good dog. He was a member of our family.

3. Barkly used to dig holes in Mom's garden. She didn't like that. It made her mad, but she still loved Barkly. He had been with us since he was a pup.

4. Barkly was always glad to see me when I came home from school. He wagged his tail and followed me around. I liked him doing that. He was a good friend.

5. Barkly was the best dog in the whole world. He did not bite anyone. He did not bark much unless he was excited.

6. Barkly's favorite toy was his blanket. It was dirty with holes in it. He dragged it all over the yard. We had to keep washing it and putting it back in his kennel. It looked like a rag, but he loved it.

7. Mom washed Barkly's blanket for me. I'm keeping it to remember what a good friend Barkly was.

Assessment

Name _____

1. What caused Barkly to die?

   (a) He was a very old dog.   (b) He ran away.

   (c) He got hit by a car.   (d) He was very sick.

2. What did Barkly do to cause Mom to get mad?

   (a) Barkly liked to chew on her clothes.

   (b) Barkly liked to dig holes in her garden.

   (c) Barkly kept running out of the gate.

   (d) Barkly liked to chew her shoes.

3. Copy words from the text to explain the effect.

   (a) I was very sad so _____.

   (b) Barkly _____ when he was excited.

   (c) Barkly's blanket was dirty and had holes in it because . . .

   _____.

Name _____

> **Remember:**
> - A fact can be checked and proven to be correct.
> - An opinion is what someone *thinks* is true and can't be proven.
> - Check all the answers before deciding.

1. Which sentence is a fact?

   (a) Barkly was a good dog.

   (b) Barkly was the best dog in the whole world.

   (c) Barkly was a very old dog.

   (d) Barkly was a good friend.

2. Which sentence is an opinion?

   (a) Barkly died at the vet's office.

   (b) Barkly was the best dog in the whole world.

   (c) Barkly used to dig holes in Mom's garden.

   (d) Barkly was a very old dog.

3. Write *fact* or *opinion* for each statement.

   (a) Barkly did not bite anyone.   _____

   (b) Barkly's blanket had holes in it.   _____

Name _____

> **Remember:**
>
> - Writers don't always tell you what they think or believe or why they have written the text. Sometimes you have to come to this conclusion based on the details given.
> - The text has details and information to find and use in making your choices. (These could be underlined.)
> - Check all answers before deciding.

1. What does the writer think about dogs?

   (a) They make a lot of noise.

   (b) They are good pets to have.

   (c) They are messy.

   (d) They can bite.

2. The writer thinks dogs make good pets because they:

   (a) drag things around.

   (b) bite people.

   (c) bark.

   (d) are like good friends.

3. Most likely, what is the best reason why the writer wrote the story?

   (a) The writer was angry.

   (b) The writer wanted to tell about Barkly.

   (c) The writer doesn't like dogs.

   (d) The writer was crying.